schools*

BUILDING ON SUCCESS

raising standards, promoting diversity, achieving results

Cm 5050   £11.45

CONTENTS

FOREWORD

This Green Paper sets out the achievements of the education service over the last few years and our plans for the years ahead. It shows how we can create an education service which plays to the strength of every individual, provides a common understanding of the knowledge base on which our society rests, promotes appreciation of the values which hold our communities together and generates the aspiration to learn from the past in order to contribute to the future. We seek to ensure that, in providing a firm grounding of accumulated knowledge, we also enable individuals to reason, to deduce, to think logically and to develop creativity. In short, we want a rounded education for every child.

In setting out plans for the future we have been careful to propose that we build on what has been achieved, see through what has begun, work in partnership with all those involved and, above all, that we are able to invest in the process of modernisation and change. By approaching reform this way we can ensure that it has a deep and lasting impact on pupil achievement and on the key goal of equality of opportunity and the development of the full potential of every young person.

David Blunkett
Secretary of State for Education and Employment

INTRODUCTION

In this Parliament we said that we would get the basics right in primary schools. We have done so. Standards of literacy and numeracy have been transformed, thanks to an historic partnership for change between teachers, parents and Government. And our pledge to cut infant class sizes of more than 30 will be delivered nationwide by this September. There is further progress to make in primary and early years provision, as set out in this paper, but the foundations are secure.

Our mission now is to bring about a similar transformation in secondary schools. This is not just a matter of new investment and individual policies to improve standards, important though these are, particularly with regard to raising the status and rewards of the teaching profession. Our primary school strategy was designed to extend the best teaching methods nationwide, based on a clear conception of the requirements of a good primary school. Our secondary strategy is similarly anchored in the achievements of the best schools today and in the requirements of a good secondary education in the knowledge economy and modern society.

Those requirements can be simply stated. Every secondary age pupil must be competent in the basics of literacy, numeracy and ICT and experience a broad curriculum beyond. Every secondary school pupil, having achieved this basic competence, must have their particular aptitudes and abilities recognised and developed to the full, particularly after the age of 14, so that they achieve good formal qualifications by the age of 16 and the means to progress beyond to further or higher education or formal work-related training. And every secondary school should instil in its pupils a strong sense of independence and responsibility, to themselves and their wider community. Our goal across education is that every boy and girl, every man and woman should have the opportunity to develop their potential to the full.

These demands are significantly greater than those made of secondary schools in the last generation, and we must be explicit in recognising the changes required of our secondary schools in consequence.

Until the very recent past, for all the ideals animating education reformers, only a minority of pupils achieved good school-leaving qualifications, while levels of drop-out and underperformance remained stubbornly high. Even today, despite real improvements since 1997 through the Excellence in Cities and specialist schools programmes, and targeted intervention in the weakest schools, fewer than half of 16 year olds achieve 5 or more good GCSEs, while levels of complete drop-out and the proportion achieving barely any qualifications, though reduced, remain unacceptably high. In last year's statutory tests for 14 year olds, just 6 in 10 were at an acceptable standard for their age in each of English, mathematics and science.

This historic poor performance was rooted in society and the economy. Parental expectations of secondary schools were generally low, particularly in regions with plentiful unskilled 'jobs for life' in the local industries. Throughout the economy the demand for skills and qualifications, and all types of further and higher education, was also far lower than today. There was general acceptance that only a minority would reach the age of 16 with significant formal skills and qualifications, particularly if destined for a vocational route beyond.

These forces shaped the comprehensive system as it developed in the 1960s and 70s. So too did the legacy of the post-1944 selective system to which the comprehensives were a reaction. Established in opposition to a very rigid and unfair system of selection between schools at the age of 11, the need to differentiate provision to individual aptitudes and abilities within schools often took second place. Inclusion too readily became an end in itself, rather than the means to identify and provide better for the talents of each individual pupil, not least those with high academic abilities and those requiring a high-quality vocational or work-related route post-14.

Furthermore, comprehensives were mostly established by local reorganisations on a model which, apart from the continuing role of Church schools and pre-existing foundations, allowed little scope for schools to develop a distinctive character and mission. Inadequate resourcing further limited the scope for schools to tailor their provision to individual needs and develop Centres of Excellence in particular areas.

Significant change is taking place on all these fronts. Expectations of pupils, and their achievements at GCSE and rates of progression to post-16 education, are rising steadily. Provision within schools is increasingly differentiated, including far more ability setting and a broadening of curriculum options. Under the influence of local management of schools and a new culture of strong school leadership by headteachers and governors, both greatly extended by this Government, schools are forging distinct missions and ethos with increasing confidence – whether as specialist schools, community or foundation schools with a particular strength and a strong sense of individual identity, or faith schools.

Schools with effective leadership and a strong sense of individual character and responsibility foster these same qualities in their pupils. Very many secondary schools now achieve high standards for many of their pupils. Under the leadership of effective headteachers, their governors and management teams, they have moved beyond the old arguments about comprehensive schools to create a system appropriate for the 21st century – embracing without reservation the principles of inclusion and equality of opportunity on which comprehensives were founded, but moving decisively beyond to tailor provision to meet the full range of individual talents, with a powerful sense of individual character and mission.

INTRODUCTION

Our ambition is to extend this best practice radically, moving the secondary system as a whole into a new era in which inclusion and equality of opportunity are a platform to promote excellence for all and to forge a strong character and ethos, school by school, focused on raising standards. Individual empowerment is the key – empowerment of each individual pupil to develop their talents to the full, and empowerment of each individual school to achieve steadily more.

We want a secondary school system in which:
- Every pupil is good at all the basics, and striving for excellence in the areas of their greatest strength.
- Every school is good at all the basics, and excellent at much more.
- Every school has a distinct mission, ethos and character, and the autonomy to manage its own affairs provided it demonstrates success.

The extension of autonomy and diversity is not an argument for a free-for-all between schools or for dismantling all local education services. As headteachers themselves recognise, certain services – such as school transport and the organisation of provision to meet children's Special Educational Needs – are essential to support the work of schools and meet the needs of pupils. Few headteachers wish to spend time organising transport. It is also vital to retain a capacity to intervene in schools whose management and standards are weak and not being improved with sufficient vigour. Freedom must be earned, not conferred at whim without regard to the interests of children or the needs of the local community.

Within this framework, there is great scope to increase school standards, autonomy and diversity, ensuring that every secondary school provides an education increasingly tailored to the needs of all its pupils. Building on the best practice of schools today, and the ambitions of our best schools for the future, this Paper sets out policies to transform secondary education over the immediate future and the medium term.

We will:

- Significantly enhance the 'earned autonomy' of successful schools, by further increasing the delegation of budgets to them, restricting needless bureaucratic burdens (including those associated with the inspection process), and by allowing them the greater freedoms over the curriculum and teachers' pay and conditions, that schools in Education Action Zones have under the 1998 legislation.

- Extend diversity within the secondary system, on the basis of high standards, by significantly expanding the specialist schools programme, welcoming more faith-based schools, continuing to establish City Academies, and changing the law to allow external sponsors to take responsibility for underperforming schools against fixed-term contracts of five to seven years with renewal subject to performance.

- Proceed with a standards drive in the early secondary years, with ambitious targets for performance in tests for 14 year olds in English, mathematics, science and ICT, with appropriate support and training for teachers and schools.

- Promote new pathways for pupils beyond 14, better suited to the talents and aspirations of individual pupils, particularly those of high ability and those wishing to proceed on vocational and work-based routes.

None of this can be achieved without sustained investment, particularly in the teaching profession and in the infrastructure – including buildings, ICT and increasing revenue budgets – essential for schools to succeed. We have made a good start here too: a capital programme trebled over the past four years, and a step-change in pay for teachers passing the new performance threshold. This Paper renews our commitment to improving the rewards and conditions of teaching, and to providing the infrastructure essential for teachers to succeed. The Prime Minister has pledged the Government to increase the share of national income devoted to education over the next five years, which will make this possible.

But investment with modernisation is the imperative. By seizing this opportunity to modernise our secondary system on the model of today's best schools, while encouraging the best to advance further and faster, we can carry through a transformation of secondary education to match the changes now progressing in primary. There is no greater mission for this Government.

CHAPTER 1
TRANSFORMING EDUCATION

OUR VISION

1.1 The Government's determination to pursue education reform and bring about a step-change in the performance of the education service has never been in doubt. Since May 1997 we have sought with passion and purpose to put into practice the Prime Minister's commitment to make education his top priority. We want a world class education service: one with standards which match the best anywhere in the world. We want them achieved not at some indeterminate future date but as soon as possible within the decade that has just begun.

1.2 Our sense of urgency comes from the belief that every passing day when a child is not able to fulfil their potential is another day lost, not only to that child but to the whole community. It comes too from the imperative for public education to prove that it can respond to the challenges of the new economy. The danger is that as the most prosperous parts of our society grow, more parents with increasing income at their disposal will turn to private education, particularly at secondary level. If this were to occur on a large scale, growing numbers of people would become less willing to pay taxes to fund public education which would then decline in quality and provide only for the disadvantaged. It is hard to imagine under those circumstances how social cohesion could be achieved and how the transmission of ever-growing inequality from one generation to the next could be avoided.

1.3 We believe, however, that successful reform is possible; that public education can meet the talents and aspirations of all students in our diverse, modern society; and that it need not take forever. The full development of the potential of every boy and girl, and every man and woman, is our goal. This is, in essence, our vision for education in England.

1.4 We now have an opportunity, possibly unique, to achieve that vision. Education is a recognised priority, not just for Government, but also for society as a whole. It is seen not only as key to developing equality of opportunity, but also to enabling the nation to prepare for the emergence of the new economy and its increased demands for skills and human capital. Expenditure on education is increasing in real terms year on year. In addition to real terms growth averaging more than 6 per cent per year between 1999–2000 and 2003–04, the Prime Minister has already promised the longest continuous rise in investment in education spending for more than a generation, with his statement that expenditure on education will rise as a proportion of national income over the next Parliament. Continuity and consistency can achieve transformation in a way that one-off bursts followed by retrenchment never could.

1.5 Furthermore, personal tax and benefit changes introduced in this Parliament will lift more than a million children out of poverty. If it is not possible to reform education successfully in these favourable circumstances, it is hard to imagine when it would be.

1.6 The Government is conscious of its starting point. In a 1995 study of adult literacy, the UK fell behind most European countries, performing similarly to the United States. At around the same time England fell below the OECD average in a study of mathematics for 13 year olds. And in 1996 fewer than six out of ten 11 year olds achieved the standards set for their age in English and mathematics.

1.7 Meanwhile, the level of participation in learning after the age of 16 was amongst the lowest in Europe, and the proportion leaving school unqualified or with low levels of qualification was unacceptably high compared to other developed countries. Furthermore, years of underperformance, conflict and poorly implemented reform had demoralised teachers and created a widespread lack of confidence in publicly-provided education.

1.8 In order to move from this starting point to the world class vision, we developed and put in place a policy approach best described as 'high challenge, high support'. This is illustrated in the diagram below.

1.9 This framework is designed to make continuous improvement for all schools in all circumstances a reality.

- The revised National Curriculum sets the standards.
- More funding is devolved to schools than in any other country, with additional funding, through programmes like Excellence in Cities, being targeted to those facing the greatest challenge.
- All schools set targets and measure their performance on the basis of excellent comparative data.
- They can easily access best practice information, for example through the Standards Site and the National Grid for Learning.
- They have increasing opportunities for professional development of staff.
- They have increased resources, and many more support staff in classrooms.
- They are held to account through inspection and the published performance tables.

- Intervention is in inverse proportion to success: schools that are underperforming are the subject of an intervention tailored to their specific circumstances; a successful school may be subject to shorter inspections, and has opportunities to lead the service, for example through becoming a Beacon school.

1.10 The emerging evidence from this country, and others where similar standards-based reforms have been made, gives us confidence that this framework for continuous school improvement is bringing rising standards and will continue to do so. It has been supported by our reforms of Local Education Authorities, which now have a clear remit to raise standards. Our principle is that schools manage schools. The Local Education Authority's job is to provide certain essential local services, and to serve as an agent for school improvement where this is not happening at school level. We have significantly increased the level of delegation of both revenue and capital direct to schools. Inspections of Local Education Authorities and the firm follow-up action we have taken where there is evidence of failure have also significantly driven up the overall level of performance.

1.11 In order to achieve a real step-change in the performance and equity of the system, we have developed and are implementing four programmes, each aligned with the framework for continuous improvement: an early years framework; the National Literacy and Numeracy Strategies at primary level; the modernisation of secondary education; and the modernisation and improvement of the teaching profession and of the context within which teaching takes place.

THE EARLY YEARS FRAMEWORK

1.12 For too long the education service failed to provide universally available early years opportunities. The degree of access depended on local provision. The voucher scheme for nursery education for 4 year olds did not solve this historic problem.

1.13 In areas of disadvantage, we have established Sure Start. So far 128 local programmes have been set up to provide support to families with children between birth and 3. Over 100,000 children are already involved, and we will extend the initiative to 500 local programmes to benefit 400,000 children under 4. This investment will make a difference to families in the short and medium term but above all it is an investment in higher school standards and greater social cohesion in ten or fifteen years time. It is a crucial step towards breaking the cycle of deprivation.

1.14 Through early years partnerships we have already put in place nursery education for all 4 year olds and are progressively making this available for all 3 year olds. We have gone further. Through co-ordinating nursery education and childcare, we are making wrap-around care available, so that parents can work, knowing that their children will be looked after throughout the day. Early Excellence Centres have been established to model best practice. The new Foundation Stage of education for ages 3 to 6 provides a set of early learning goals and better continuity between the early years and school. New inspection arrangements will ensure that all early years settings are of real quality. As a result, more children than ever will arrive at school ready to learn. Our plans for building on these achievements are set out in Chapter 2.

THE NATIONAL LITERACY AND NUMERACY STRATEGIES IN PRIMARY SCHOOLS

1.15 Our education system will never be world class unless virtually all children learn to read, write and calculate to high standards before they leave primary school.

1.16 We have therefore given top priority to a national strategy to achieve this goal, setting ambitious national targets for 2002: that in English 80 per cent and in mathematics 75 per cent of 11 year olds should meet the standards set for their age. These targets are staging posts on the way to even higher levels of performance. To achieve them we have progressively put in place what the leading Canadian educator, Michael Fullan, has called among the most ambitious, comprehensive and aligned national strategies anywhere in the world. Primary teachers, heads and support staff have responded magnificently.

1.17 Their impact is evident in the national test results over the last three years. The excellent progress so far is only the beginning. Our intention is to pursue the strategies consistently, to refine them and to invest in professional development for primary teachers through to 2004 at least. Our plans for enabling primary schools to advance beyond their current remarkable achievements are set out in Chapter 3.

THE MODERNISATION OF SECONDARY EDUCATION

1.18 Our drive for world class performance demands that we modernise secondary education so that it builds on rather than dissipates the growing success of the primary sector. We need our best schools to strive harder still. We need all pupils to be achieving as highly as they are able. We also need to narrow the achievement gap both between schools in disadvantaged areas and those elsewhere and between schools which have succeeded against the odds and those with historically low levels of achievement. Over the last two years, through the early implementation of Excellence in Cities and the pilot of our programme to raise standards for 11–14 year olds, we have made a start. All the evidence suggests that there has been improvement at secondary level but there is much more to do.

1.19 Bringing about a step-change at secondary level is the top priority for the next phase of reform. A major transformation is planned, both of the transition from primary to secondary school and of the quality of teaching and learning in both lower and upper secondary education. We plan to ensure that each secondary school is excellent in providing the central core of learning but also has a clear mission and ethos, so that it makes its own distinctive contribution. Our proposals are set out in Chapter 4.

THE MODERNISATION OF THE TEACHING PROFESSION

1.20 The success of the Literacy and Numeracy Strategies shows what teachers can achieve when they have the right support. It proves too that no matter how coherent our framework for school improvement, no matter how successful our policies to strengthen primary and secondary education, world class standards will elude us unless we can recruit, retain, develop and motivate teachers and school leaders of real quality.

1.21 There is a justified belief that society does not value teachers sufficiently. If economic success continues, the education service will be competing ever more fiercely with growing demands for talented graduates. For all these reasons we developed in the *Teachers* Green Paper in December 1998 the most radical reform of the teaching profession since the Second World War. At the heart of this reform are measures, still being implemented, for paying teachers better, for providing them with more support in the classroom and for investing more in their initial training and professional development, so that we recruit and retain good quality teachers.

1.22 We want teachers to be able to concentrate on teaching, planning, assessing and their own professional development and to be freed from other tasks by support staff and by information technology-based systems. At times, our reforms have created increased workload and administrative burdens. We have begun to address this, by reducing dramatically the need for schools to bid for funds and cutting very sharply the paperwork sent to schools. Last term we achieved a two-thirds cut in the number of documents sent to secondary schools and a 40 per cent cut for primary schools, compared to the same term last year, but this is only a start.

1.23 The steps we have taken so far to implement these reforms and our plan to build on them to help teachers to meet the challenges of the 21st century are set out in Chapter 5.

OUR ACHIEVEMENTS SO FAR: THE EVIDENCE

1.24 When we published the *Excellence in Schools* White Paper in July 1997, we set out a clear agenda. We have stuck to it firmly and, taken together, the reforms of that Paper are delivering significant results.

1.25 Among the key achievements are the following.

- Universal nursery education for all 4 year olds has been put in place. There has been a significant expansion for 3 year olds. In total there are 120,000 more free nursery places now than in 1997.
- 298,000 new childcare places, created between April 1997 and September 2000, have provided care for more than 546,000 children. Taking into account turnover, this has added more than 182,000 places to the stock of childcare places available across England, helping more than 343,000 children.
- Infant class sizes have been cut. Almost half a million children were in infant classes of more than 30 in January 1998. By September 2000 the number was just 30,000. The Government's election pledge that no 5, 6 or 7 year old would be in a class of more than 30 will be met ahead of schedule in September 2001, as a result of our investment of £620 million.
- The primary pupil:teacher ratio improved between 1998 and 2000 from 23.7 to 23.3, after years of steady increases.
- There is more money going into schools. In 2000–01, we are spending over £300 more per pupil in real terms than in 1997–98. In total over the next three years we are spending a further £370 per pupil, taking the total increase to around £700 per pupil between 1997–98 and 2003–04.

- Investment in school building has tripled – from £683 million in 1996–97 to £2.1 billion in 2000–01. Over the next three years there is a further £7.8 billion. By 2003-04 we will be spending £3.2 billion a year on schools capital, including £500 million of funding devolved to schools to spend as they choose. In the next three years, we will be making available almost £1 billion in devolved capital – 40 per cent more than the total capital spend on schools in 1996–97. Around 17,000 schools – three-quarters of all schools – are already benefiting from New Deal for Schools grant funding.
- A programme of action for children with Special Educational Needs was outlined in the 1997 Green Paper *Excellence for All Children* and has been implemented.
- Investment improving the accessibility of schools for children with Special Educational Needs has been increased substantially from £4 million in 1997–98 to £30 million this year, and £220 million over the next three years.
- Thousands of schools are now working towards the National Healthy School Standard, and all Education Authorities are engaged in successful partnerships with their local health authority to support this work. The Department of Health and DfEE are jointly providing £5.7 million of funding annually for this programme.
- A total of 20,200 schools (98 per cent of secondary and 86 per cent of primary schools) are now connected to the Internet, compared to around 6,500 in 1998.
- There is now one computer for every 8 pupils in secondary schools and one for every 13 in primary schools (compared to an average of 9 secondary and 18 primary pupils sharing a computer in 1998). The directly-managed part of the National Grid for Learning website receives some 2.5 million hits each week.

- Dissemination of best practice has improved. The Standards Site (a best practice website) received 64 million hits last year. Already 550 Beacon schools are in operation and around 4,000 excellent primary teachers are funded to model best practice in the teaching of English and mathematics.
- We have reduced paperwork for teachers – cutting by a third the number of documents we send to schools this year, and radically simplifying the Standards Fund, with no more bidding and streamlined monitoring. And the number of classroom assistants supporting teachers has increased by 24,000.
- Over 450 Learning Support Units [LSUs] have been established to date in Excellence in Cities areas, including 59 pilot primary LSUs to enable schools to tackle the problems of disruptive pupils without excluding them. We will provide £11 million in 2000–01 and £17 million in 2001–02 for up to 360 LSUs in areas outside the Excellence in Cities programme. We aim to have over 1,000 in place by 2002. As a result of these and similar targeted actions, the number of exclusions was cut by 15 per cent from 1997–98 to 1998–99.

1.26 These dramatic changes in the inputs are crucial but improvements in teaching quality and pupil outcomes must be the acid test of our reforms. The evidence shows just how much progress has been made. The policies and the investments are combining to deliver higher quality and higher standards.

- There are now fewer unsatisfactory lessons: according to OFSTED figures the percentage is down to 6 per cent from around 20 per cent in 1994–95.
- There are fewer failing schools: over 650 have been successfully turned around since 1997. Importantly too OFSTED has shown that once schools emerge from special measures they continue to improve.
- Fewer schools are going into special measures: only 48 in autumn 2000 compared to 69 in the equivalent term in 1999. The measures we have put in place are preventing as well as curing failure.
- More children leave primary school able to read and write well. Seventy-five per cent of children achieved Level 4 in 2000 compared to just 57 per cent in 1996: that is 160,000 more children meeting the standard than four years ago.
- More children leave primary school numerate. Seventy-two per cent achieved Level 4 in 2000 compared to 54 per cent in 1996: 155,000 more children meeting the standard than four years ago.
- Progress in primary school English and mathematics is fastest in the most disadvantaged areas of the country. The lowest scoring Local Education Authority in Key Stage 2 English is now doing better than the national average of four years ago.
- More young people achieve 5 or more higher grades at GCSE – 49.2 per cent in 2000 compared to 46.3 per cent in 1998.
- Exam and test results in the Excellence in Cities areas are improving more quickly than in other places – with a rise of 2.3 percentage points between 1999 and 2000 in those getting 5 good GCSEs, compared to 1.3 percentage points in other areas.
- The biggest jump in standards within those cities is at the most deprived schools.
- Results for 11 year olds in the 25 round one Education Action Zones improved more than national results in 2000. In English, mathematics and science the increase between 1998 and 2000 in the numbers meeting national standards was 11, 16 and 20 percentage points respectively (compared with 10, 13 and 15 percentage points nationally).

- In specialist schools, the proportion of pupils achieving 5 or more A*– C GCSE grades increased by 6.1 percentage points between 1997 and 2000, half as much again as in other schools.
- The percentage of black pupils achieving 5 or more A*– Cs at GCSE rose far faster than the national average between 1998 and 2000.
- The percentage of children of parents whose occupation is 'unskilled or semi-skilled manual' achieving 5 or more A*– Cs at GCSE also rose far faster than the national average.
- Performance at A level and in vocational qualifications has risen steadily too throughout the last four years.
- The number of young people leaving school with no qualifications at all has fallen from 45,000 in 1997 to 33,000 in 2000.

1.27 Perhaps most importantly of all there are two further underlying achievements. The first is that the education service has demonstrated over the last three and a half years that rapid, fundamental reform, which really makes a difference to children and young people, is possible. The old sense of despair, which used to bedevil education, is increasingly being replaced by precisely the 'can-do' culture we advocated in the 1997 White Paper.

1.28 The second is that the education service has a culture focused, as never before, on standards and targets. Teachers seek out what works, and believe in their capacity to make a difference to the life chances of pupils. There is some way to go before teachers – and society as a whole – realise the extent of the shift. But make no mistake: teachers, with governors and other school staff, are making real progress. These achievements provide the foundation for the next phase of our education revolution.

A STRATEGIC APPROACH TO REFORM

1.29 In the succeeding chapters, we look at what we have achieved and what we propose for the next stage of reform phase by phase. However, our proposals for each phase of the school system are based on a common set of eight strategic intentions which were discussed with thousands of headteachers in a series of consultative conferences in autumn 2000 and refined to take account of their feedback.

1. WE WILL SEE THINGS THROUGH AND BUILD ON THE ACHIEVEMENTS SO FAR.

Over the next three to five years our first priority is to make sure that our current reforms become irreversible. Modernisation and consistency go hand in hand. In the past and in other countries, promising education reforms have all too often failed because governments did not see them through until they had a deep and lasting impact on performance. As a result, frustration built up among teachers: their work in bringing about change was so often wasted. And the credibility of reform itself was called into question.

Society cannot afford to make these mistakes again. Our reforms in the last three and a half years have brought undoubted progress. Teachers have invested great skill and commitment in the success that has been achieved but they know, and we know, that there is much more to do. Our first priority must be to complete what we have begun. Continuity and consistency are crucial. For example, the Literacy and Numeracy Strategies at primary level need further investment and further refinement at least until 2004 to ensure that standards continue to rise. Similarly, the reforms of the teaching profession begun in the last three years need to be firmly embedded.

Where we need to refine existing policies in the light of experience or to make progress with the next stage of reform, we will do so in ways that recognise, reinforce and embed further the progress that has been made. In short, we will seek consistency, stability and continued improvement.

2. WE WILL CONTINUE TO PROMOTE HIGH STANDARDS AND NARROW INEQUALITIES IN ACHIEVEMENT BETWEEN ADVANTAGED AND DISADVANTAGED AREAS, GROUPS AND INDIVIDUALS.

We want a publicly-provided education service for everyone. School by school, we must press for higher standards at the top, and steadily increase the proportion achieving at the highest level. We must also focus on raising the 'floor' level of achievement. Pupils from disadvantaged backgrounds need better opportunities to succeed: the school system should be the decisive factor in unlocking their potential and giving them the opportunity to fulfil their ambitions.

In practical terms this means that we need a faster rate of improvement in disadvantaged areas than in others and within all areas faster improvement for the most disadvantaged children; at least equal improvements in boys' performance as in girls'; faster progress than often in the past for pupils from some ethnic minority groups; and continued practical support for all pupils with Special Educational Needs. Achieving these goals requires that we co-ordinate education policy with other strategies to challenge generational and historic disadvantage, lack of economic activity and a poor physical environment. Our policies for economic and social regeneration and for the family and community are key to ensuring success.

It also means that we need universal policies, which include every school, as well as targeted, extra support to those schools and pupils that face the greatest challenge in achieving high standards. A number of current policies, including the Literacy and Numeracy Strategies, Education Action Zones, Excellence in Cities, the promotion of out-of-school learning, improved provision for pupils with Special Educational Needs and the Ethnic Minority Achievement Grant are designed to provide this extra support. The tests and examinations in 2000 and the Youth Cohort Study indicate that, at last, achievement differences are beginning to narrow. Building on this early progress is a key priority.

3. WE WILL TAILOR EDUCATION TO THE TALENTS, ASPIRATIONS AND POTENTIAL OF INDIVIDUAL PUPILS.

In the 20th century, our education service was too often built on a 'one size fits all' model. In the 21st century we need to change this and build a flexible system around the needs and aspirations of individual pupils and their families, particularly at secondary level. The reforms of the last few years have laid the foundations for this shift. Individual pupil-level target-setting has become accepted practice in many primary and secondary schools; Learning Mentors provide assistance to individual pupils with challenges outside school; subject by subject setting enables teachers to meet the talents of individual pupils more effectively; schools are increasingly using data systems which enable individual pupil progress to be tracked; and Information and Communications Technology (ICT) opens up a wealth of opportunity for pupils to take greater control of their own learning and study minority subjects (such as Latin or Japanese) which might not have been available in the past. Building on these developments is a major theme throughout this Paper.

4. WE WILL OFFER THE OPPORTUNITY OF HIGH STANDARDS IN BOTH ACADEMIC AND VOCATIONAL SUBJECTS AND ENCOURAGE 'EDUCATION WITH CHARACTER'.

The importance of high academic standards is widely accepted and has been the central thrust of our school reforms. By encouraging greater opportunities for work-related learning for pupils aged 14 upwards and by enabling schools to vary the curriculum for 14–16 year olds and offer more vocational options, we have also done a great deal to encourage vocational education. What matters most however is that vocational qualifications are of comparable standard to their academic counterparts and that their status is respected by employers, parents and students.

In addition, we want to establish 'education with character' in every school. This phrase is intended to suggest that pupils, in addition to achieving high standards, should have the opportunity at school to develop as well-rounded, creative, self-reliant individuals, who know right from wrong, who can work in teams, who respect their fellow pupils whatever their backgrounds, who are able to manage their own learning, who see the value of working hard now in order to achieve success later, who are prepared to take risks, who are steadfast in the face of adversity and who have the confidence to contribute to the success of their school, their families and their community. These characteristics are as important in the workplace as they are in the community and are highly prized by employers.

Character building is a key part of an overall approach to education which values scholarship, endeavour and the idea of a citizen of the future who is self-reliant and simultaneously able to contribute to the wider community.

5. WE WILL ENCOURAGE INNOVATION, ENABLE SCHOOLS TO USE INFORMATION AND COMMUNICATIONS TECHNOLOGY TO TRANSFORM TEACHING AND LEARNING AND MODEL THE SCHOOL OF THE FUTURE.

The application of ICT is transforming business processes in every sector of the economy, both private and public. It is beginning to have a similar impact in education. Indeed, in some schools, the transformative power of ICT has already been unleashed. Many of the case studies in this document are testimony to that.

The next challenge is to extend the benefits of ICT to all schools, while creating a culture in education which encourages innovation and therefore constantly challenges inherited attitudes and approaches in the pursuit of higher standards.

To achieve these goals demands investment in infrastructure and in digital resources. But technology is only a tool: the key to innovation is teachers and other staff with the confidence and skills to exploit its potential to transform the learning process and motivate children to learn. Just as importantly, schools, often working together, must have the freedom to innovate and the confidence to do so.

6. WE WILL ENCOURAGE DIVERSITY AMONG SECONDARY SCHOOLS, EXTEND AUTONOMY FOR SUCCESSFUL SCHOOLS AND INTERVENE ONLY IN INVERSE PROPORTION TO SUCCESS.

Since 1997 we have applied our policy of intervention in inverse proportion to success. We have targeted underperformance wherever it has occurred, whether at school or Local Authority level. As performance has improved, we have also given the vast majority of schools much greater autonomy especially over funding. No other education service in the world devolves as much power and responsibility to schools as we do. Increasingly, too, we have introduced rewards and opportunity for successful schools to lead the system. Giving schools greater freedom and encouraging them to play to their strengths has brought a welcome diversity to publicly-provided education. The evidence suggests that schools with a distinctive ethos and mission are more likely to succeed. Promoting diversity leads to greater flexibility, more opportunities for schools to learn from each other and, above all, a wider range of opportunities and choices for pupils and parents.

Our vision is of confident, successful schools which develop a distinct mission and ethos and welcome the opportunity to contribute to the improvement of the whole system, to share best practice and to work in partnership.

7. WE WILL DEMONSTRATE TRUST IN THE INFORMED PROFESSIONAL JUDGEMENT OF TEACHERS WHILE MAINTAINING A FOCUS ON ACCOUNTABILITY AND STANDARDS.

Schools are more firmly focused on pupil performance than ever before. They have demonstrated their capacity to make a difference and the teaching profession has embraced accountability more than any other.

As a result, teachers have become determined to seek out best practice and apply it in their classrooms and schools. Meanwhile, through a range of policies, including the establishment of Beacon schools, Internet best practice sites and investment in professional development, we have made it easier than ever to find and apply best practice. In these circumstances, the key to improvement school by school, classroom by classroom is the informed professional judgement of staff.

Increasingly, the Government will involve those working in schools in designing, implementing and refining policy. We will build on the experience of policies such as Excellence in Cities which have been implemented in partnership with schools.

8. WE WILL ENCOURAGE PARTNERSHIPS BETWEEN THE EDUCATION SERVICE AND ALL THOSE WHO HAVE AN INTEREST IN ITS SUCCESS.

We will encourage those within the education service to learn from each other and to work with and learn from those outside it – parents, communities, the cultural sector and business. The growth of learning opportunities at home and in the community, spurred on by dramatic technological change, increases the need for educators to work with all kinds of partners. In this way the education service can not only learn from experience of change and progress elsewhere, it can also become a valued possession of society as a whole: a public service, which is absolutely central to the creation of a successful economy and society in the future.

1.30 The remainder of this document sets out how we intend to put these principles into practice over the next few years.

CHAPTER 2
EARLY YEARS

FOR EARLY EDUCATION AND CHILDCARE

We will:

- provide free nursery places for two-thirds of 3 year olds by March 2002 and for all who want one by September 2004; provide new childcare places benefiting 1 million children by 2004; and helping to stimulate an extra 100,000 full-time places for children of nursery school age, linking education with childcare;
- fund 500 Sure Start programmes to support 400,00 under 4s, one-third of under 4s living in poverty by 2004; increase the number of Early Excellence Centres to 100 and create up to 900 Neighbourhood Nursery Centres in disadvantaged areas by 2004;
- improve quality, so that by 2004 virtually all provision is satisfactory or better; and introduce a star-rating scheme to provide better information for parents, enhance choice and raise standards; and
- invest further in the Foundation Stage, ensuring four days training each year for all and developing links with infant education; introduce a professional qualification in early years and childcare; enable up to 1,000 people to qualify as teachers through new routes; and provide training so that all providers have a trained Special Educational Needs co-ordinator with expert back-up.

THERE IS ALREADY BETTER SUPPORT FOR FAMILIES AND MORE PROVISION...

2.1 Children's experiences in the earliest years of their life are critical to their subsequent development. They have a significant impact on their future performance at school and the extent to which they are able to take advantage of opportunities later in life. That is why we have invested heavily in early years education and why our programmes from birth onwards support children and their parents and continue to support them right through to the start of formal education and beyond. It is also why this Government has begun a drive to halve child poverty in 10 years and to eradicate it in 20.

2.2 Traditionally early years services have been delivered separately by a range of professionals working in distinct education, care and health services. However, very young children do not distinguish between care and education, and families' needs in the modern world are best met by providing joined-up services. Our approach to early years education and care is to develop seamless services for children and families. We want to retain the best which each profession offers, but provide more integrated services which are built around children's needs rather than professional structures. All the evidence shows that joined-up services deliver both better outcomes for children and better value for the public purse.

THE PEEP PROJECT

2.3 We have introduced the Sure Start programme, to ensure that children and families in disadvantaged areas have access to the services, opportunities and practical help which enable young children to flourish from birth. Sure Start promotes the physical, intellectual, social and emotional development of young children through a range of education, parent support and health services so that they are ready to succeed when they start school.

2.4 It supports parents and children with enhanced childcare, play and early learning opportunities and better access to health services – from ante-natal and baby clinics to specialist services for children with Special Educational Needs. Services are delivered in new ways, by staff working together across health, care and education. We will have invested £452 million in the programme by April 2002, establishing 128 local programmes, with over 100,000 children already involved. Local Sure Start programmes are led by local partnerships with strong parental and community involvement.

2.5 A range of other programmes are being developed (including, for example, providing books for babies) which support parents in bringing up their children (see The PEEP Project, for example). By helping to provide a good start in life, children will benefit as they move into early education and then into more formal education.

The Peers in Early Education Project (PEEP) was set up to improve the life chances of children in disadvantaged areas in the Blackbird Leys, Rose Hill and Littlemore estates in south-east Oxford. It aims to help improve children's educational attainment, especially in literacy, by supporting parents and carers in their role as first educators.

From birth to school it offers materials, group sessions and home visits to parents and carers. The focus is on listening, talking, playing and singing together and sharing books every day, aiming to lay the foundations for later learning, especially literacy. PEEP also collaborates with pre-school settings and primary schools as the basis for long-term home-school partnerships beginning in the Foundation Stage.

Early evaluation findings indicate that PEEP makes a positive impact on babies' and young children's development and on parents and carers in their role as first educators.

PARENTS AS PARTNERS

Parents as Partners brings together adults and children in severely deprived areas of Sheffield to develop their skills, build confidence and raise aspirations. There are three types of activity: parents and children learning together (for example in literacy, numeracy and communication); parents learning together (for example, computing for beginners); and children learning together, eg at the after-school club which their parents run. The Workers' Educational Association established the project six years ago at Wybourn Community Primary School. Now its activities cover six local schools and help over 200 people a year. Parents as Partners has become a firmly established part of the community, with funding from a range of sources including the Local Authority and the DfEE.

Chris McKee, the Parents as Partners co-ordinator, has been employed by the initiative from the outset. She said: "Family learning – it's bigger than individuals. There's a roll-on effect out into the community."

2.6 Our support for families includes support for family learning. Family learning also benefits adults – a child's first chance to learn may be a parent's second. It can develop adults' skills, improve their chances of employment and give them the confidence to continue learning. Our support has included:

- Family Literacy and Numeracy: we are supporting courses for some 20,000 families in 2000–01; with an additional £10 million to reach a further 50,000 parents and 22,000 children. Family Literacy and Numeracy will be a key part of the national adult basic skills strategy we plan to launch this spring.
- The Adult and Community Learning Fund (ACLF) – family learning is one of the themes of this £20 million challenge fund which supports small-scale local projects to take learning into sectors of the community rarely reached by traditional educational institutions (see Parents as Partners, for example).

2.7 An evaluation of our national Family Literacy initiative by the National Foundation for Educational Research (NFER) has shown:

- An increase in employment – from 19 per cent of parents in work to 43 per cent at the end of their courses, the majority of whom attributed their employment to Family Literacy.
- An increase in parents' learning – in 1997, 60 per cent went on to take a further course of study, compared to none in 1994.

2.8 Critical though this support is for disadvantaged families, it must be backed up by high-quality early education for all, if children are to be able to take full advantage of their future formal education. In the past, Britain's investment in early years education lagged behind that of our competitor nations and early education was much more readily available in some parts of the country than in others. We have therefore taken steps to expand our investment, to ensure that it is consistently available everywhere and have abolished the divisive nursery voucher scheme. We have introduced local partnerships working for the benefit of all families, parents and children to develop a planned approach to early years development and childcare, with a choice of provision for parents.

2.9 Since September 1998, there has been a free early education place for every 4 year old whose parents want one. By March 2002 two-thirds of 3 year olds will have a free place and, in total, some 120,000 new, free early education places have been created since 1997. Over the next year alone, we will be investing £250 million in early education provision.

2.10 In the past, the quality of early education was patchy – there was much excellent, but also some unsatisfactory, provision. Clearly it is the quality of a child's early years education which will determine the benefit to the child of that experience. To support our quality agenda we have introduced a distinct early years phase, the Foundation Stage, covering children from the age of 3 to the end of their reception year in primary school, and Early Learning Goals, setting out what the majority of children should achieve by the end of their reception year.

2.11 These are major advances, which few other countries yet have in place. OFSTED has found that the quality of nursery education has improved markedly. In March 1998, only 66 per cent of provision was judged to be acceptable; by March 2000 OFSTED found that 89 per cent met an acceptable standard. Parents can increasingly be assured that children will learn through play with enjoyment and challenge, and that a framework is in place to enable children to acquire those key skills, such as listening, speaking, concentrating and working as a group, which make for later effective learning.

2.12 We have supported this new phase by providing resources for training and developing nursery staff. Local Education Authorities are also investing in this phase of education and recognise the benefits of providing children with high-quality early learning experiences.

2.13 Early identification of children's Special Educational Needs is a key part of our early years strategy. The earlier we can identify and support a child's needs, the greater the likelihood of that child developing their full potential. There is also evidence that early intervention will enhance the child's chances of being able to be educated in mainstream schooling. We have introduced measures to ensure that SEN is identified as early as possible, and assessed sensitively by the appropriate qualified professionals, and now require Early Years Partnerships to develop strategies for children with SEN.

THOMAS CORAM EARLY EXCELLENCE CENTRE

The Coram Community Campus provides a one-stop shop for local parents and children, drawing together a range of services. The Early Excellence Centre is a partnership between Camden Local Authority and Coram Family, the children's charity. The Centre has 108 children undertaking nursery education, and 400 families use the campus each week. The key factors in its high quality provision include the following:

• Parents are involved in all aspects of children's learning. When a child is offered a place, parents are involved in assessing their child's current level of understanding across the curriculum. Learning priorities are set for each child, and staff and parents regularly review progress. Children help

to assess their work and choose samples of it for inclusion in their portfolios. Staff meet at the end of each day to evaluate and plan the children's work against learning intentions. Parents also attend groups on different aspects of the curriculum and practical workshops.

• Full inclusion of children with SEN and children in need. The expertise of a range of practitioners, such as speech therapists, health visitors, social workers and clinical psychologists, is used to ensure that there is a comprehensive assessment and detailed plan for each child. The campus also hosts KIDS, a charity which provides support for children with SEN.

- A strong emphasis on creativity. Children are encouraged to develop their creativity using a wide range of resources and equipment. They have worked on innovative projects with a variety of outside experts, including musicians, dancers, an architecture student, artists and music teachers.

- Extensive community links, including a drop-in centre which also provides outreach, a toy library and works with parents in local primary schools. There are classes every afternoon for parents and carers in, for example, effective parenting. Childminders study for qualifications in Childcare and Education.

2.14 As part of our effort to support integration of early education with day care and to spread good practice we have developed a pilot programme of 29 Early Excellence Centres (EECs) delivering high-quality integrated early education, childcare, family support services and training opportunities from the same site. Early findings from the evaluation of the Early Excellence Programme suggests significant benefits to children and their families. We have also found that for every £1 spent on joined-up services in EECs, £8 is saved in alternative services. The Parents as Partners study described earlier illustrates the work that one such centre is carrying out.

2.15 We are also introducing National Standards for the regulation of day care to ensure consistent quality across the country. In future, OFSTED will inspect childcare as well as early education provision, furthering our vision of seamless provision. As well as supporting improvements in quality, this will reduce the regulatory burden in many cases, since early education provision will now face only one rather than two inspections.

... BUT WE NEED TO DO MORE TO ACHIEVE OUR AMBITIONS

2.16 We have made a tremendous start on a challenging agenda. We have made major improvements in the amount of provision and the quality of services provided. We have made great strides in integrating services ever more effectively with related agencies and service providers. But we know that we need to do much more if we are to achieve our ambitions for early education and childcare.

2.17 First, we will continue to extend the Sure Start programme, initially to 500 local programmes, so that it reaches 400,000 under 4s, a third of all children under 4 living in poverty. The support provided by Sure Start includes significant opportunities for adult learning and support for parenting, leading to real gains in the development of children. It supports the Government's drives to eradicate child poverty and to create an equal start in life. In total, we will be investing £500 million each year by 2003–04.

2.18 We will encourage the development of new integrated early years centres which draw on the strengths of the public, private and voluntary sectors. Through the Early Excellence Centre programme, Sure Start, Neighbourhood Nursery centres and other programmes we will create, and encourage others to create, up to 100,000 new full-time nursery education places where childcare is available to cover a normal or extended day. Many of these places will also provide for children aged under 3.

2.19 Research shows that children are eager and highly capable learners between birth and the age of 3. For these youngest children, we also want to build on our work with parents, in particular by extending family learning programmes, recognising the evidence that early reading activity in the home is a key to later success. We will therefore develop a framework of best practice for supporting children between these ages.

2.20 Recent research highlights the very strong link between the shared reading and literacy activities of parent and child and later attainment. We want to build on this, drawing on the excellent work done in projects such as PEEP in Oxford (see page 19) and parental support strategies at Early Excellence Centres such as Pen Green in Corby. We will also continue to support Home Start, which provides valuable assistance to families at times of particular stress. All our activity in this area will be aimed at supporting the youngest children and their parents.

2.21 Secondly, we will steadily extend early education provision, so that from September 2004, every 3 year old whose parents want one will have a free nursery place. In total, we will invest some £390 million by 2003–04 to provide universal pre-school education for 3 and 4 year olds, thus completing a transformation talked about for 30 years, but never previously carried out. It will be based on partnerships between the public, private and voluntary sectors – so that parents have a real choice of early education provision, including playgroups and public and private sector nurseries.

2.22 The National Childcare Strategy aims to ensure that affordable, accessible, quality childcare is available in every neighbourhood for working families and their children. By March 2004, the goal is to have created places for 1.6 million children: a million more children being provided with childcare than ever before, taking into account turnover. Employment levels in this sector already grew more in absolute terms between spring 1997 and spring 2000 than in any other and we estimate that at least 150,000 new people will need to be recruited by March 2004 for this further expansion.

2.23 Over the next three years, the Government will be providing extra help to start up childcare in disadvantaged areas, which will include establishing 45,000 new nursery places in up to 900 Neighbourhood Nursery Centres. Many of these will bring together services for families and children through combined nursery education, childcare and family support. The Government is committed to joining up funding streams as far as possible for childcare, nursery education and other programmes targeted on families and disadvantaged areas so that services are integrated and bureaucracy for providers is reduced. One hundred and forty-five thousand new childminder places will also be started up by March 2004 and 450 networks will be established to support childminders.

2.24 Thirdly, we will continue to push up the quality of provision. By 2004, virtually all early years provision will provide satisfactory or better progress towards the Early Learning Goals. Any that do not will have to put in place a clear improvement plan. We will continue to develop the Foundation Stage as a distinct phase, so that, before entry to Year 1, children work towards the Early Learning Goals in specialist early years provision, taught by specialist early years practitioners.

2.25 We will develop a national quality star-rating scheme, which signals good quality care and learning for children, inspires the confidence of parents, and is seen as good for business by providers. By building on existing accreditation schemes we will create a rigorous evaluation process, which will encourage providers to raise standards and enable parents to make informed choices for their children.

2.26 We will promote the development of excellence through an expansion of Early Excellence Centres, which both provide integrated early education and childcare, and develop and spread best practice. Our aim is to have 100 centres by 2004. We will also support nursery schools in developing a wider range of services so as to serve their community more broadly. We aim to help 250 schools in this way by 2004.

2.27 There will be much greater investment in training the workforce. It is critical that those working with young children are trained to high professional standards, and that qualifications support the development of an integrated sector. The new Learning and Skills Council has already been set a target to give 230,000 people new or higher childcare qualifications by March 2004 and will be working with local partnerships to achieve this. We will plan closer integration of qualifications for early years and childcare workers, building on work that has already been done. This will enable people to move around the system more easily and to progress in manageable steps. Although some qualifications may still focus on one aspect of care and early education, we will bring them closer together, for example, by requiring common modules, so that all individuals train in important common areas. And we will ensure that all early years practitioners have the benefit of at least four days training each year, to support their work with children in the Foundation Stage.

2.28 We also want more early education specialists to come through teacher training. We will work on new routes into teaching and other senior early years practitioner posts so as to make the best of the skills and experience of the very large early years and childcare workforce. By 2004 we will support up to 1,000 people in obtaining qualified teacher status or senior practitioner status through our new framework of qualifications. We will also ensure that good quality leadership training is available to those in or aspiring to leadership positions in the sector.

2.29 In introducing the Foundation Stage, we made a clear commitment to support the early identification of Special Educational Needs (SEN) and to improve the prospects of children with SEN. This is central to our approach to the early years. We are working closely with the health and social services to ensure that medical and social services staff can work sensitively and effectively with young children and their parents. We will make significant resources available over the next three years to help ensure that all staff delivering the Foundation Stage are equipped to meet this key priority. This includes training for SEN Co-ordinators (SENCOs) working in the early years.

2.30 By 2004, Early Years Development and Childcare Partnerships will ensure that everywhere providing early education will have access to a trained SENCO. We have set a target for 2004 of one area co-ordinator for every 20 providers. These area co-ordinators will support providers and make the necessary links to specialist services provided by the Local Education Authority and other agencies. And we will look for means of helping to develop the services offered by Local Authorities to parents and children whose Special Educational Needs are identified in their very early years.

WE WILL CREATE A SMOOTHER TRANSITION INTO SCHOOL

2.31 As the Foundation Stage and Early Learning Goals become embedded in our education system, it is critical that the transition between early education and the greater formality of school is made smoothly. We want to work with headteachers and teachers to develop the full potential of this new and distinct phase in education and to build strong and clear links with infant education. We want to support the development of more provision which sees children through the whole Foundation Stage in one place, to improve continuity and enhance parental choice.

2.32 We will also work to improve contact between primary schools and the early years, improving records transfer, and encouraging clusters of early years providers to link to schools. In the longer term, other forms of co-operative working, including staff exchanges and joint approaches to professional development can also be used to ease the transition. Early years services will continue to be incorporated into our targeted programmes, such as Excellence in Cities and Education Action Zones.

2.33 This important investment in the early years of a child's education is vital to our ambition of enabling every child to develop their potential. By expanding services, promoting greater integration of early years services and enhancing the quality of services, children will begin their primary education better equipped than ever before.

CHAPTER 3
PRIMARY EDUCATION TRANSFORMED

IN PRIMARY SCHOOLS

We will:

• achieve our targets for English and mathematics at 11 – that 80 per cent achieve the standard set for their age (Level 4 or above) in English and 75 per cent in mathematics by 2002;

• consult on targets for 2004 that 85 per cent of 11 year olds achieve the standard set for their age in English and in mathematics, and that 35 per cent achieve the advanced Level 5 in each subject; and

• make sure that every child receives a rounded and enriched education, with a broad curriculum and opportunities for extra-curricular activities, including access to sport, the arts and to citizenship programmes.

TRANSFORMATION HAS BEGUN ...

3.1 At primary school, the essential building blocks of future learning, including reading, writing and arithmetic need to be established. That is why we have given the highest possible priority to raising standards of achievement in the basics for all primary pupils. The investment of an average of £190 million each year for the next three years in the National Literacy and Numeracy Strategies, on top of other increases in resources for primary schools, shows how great a priority this remains. The strategies must be seen through and have a deep and irreversible impact on pupil performance.

3.2 The wholehearted commitment of governors, teachers and non-teaching staff across the country has been the key to the success so far in raising standards of English and mathematics. Every day, in all 18,000 primary schools, they are using their professionalism to take forward the national strategies and integrate them within the wider curriculum. All the evidence shows that primary heads and teachers are now enthusiastically committed to the teaching methods they have learnt from the national strategies, not least because they can see they make a real difference to what their children achieve. In a survey of Year 4 and 5 teachers 91 per cent said that they supported the principle of a National Literacy Strategy and 75 per cent said that they enjoyed teaching it. Ninety-seven per cent supported the principle of a National Numeracy Strategy and 92 per cent enjoyed teaching the daily mathematics lesson. The Literacy Hour and daily mathematics lesson have also been immensely popular with parents. The standards achieved in mathematics (across the board, and not just in mental arithmetic) have risen sharply. And the appreciation of all kinds of writing including poetry, fiction and non-fiction has improved dramatically. Writing too is beginning to improve especially among young children. Cleeve Primary School (see page 30) is a dramatic example of what schools have achieved.

3.3 A key part of the strategies has been the high-quality training in best practice provided for all teachers and headteachers in every primary school. We introduced changes to initial teacher training for new teachers and suitable in-service training for serving teachers to support the Strategies. As a result, all teachers are able to teach English and mathematics in the ways that have been proven to work best. Teaching assistants too have been involved as an important part of this process.

3.4 The figure below shows how nationally the number of 11 year olds achieving the standard expected for their age (Level 4 or above) has risen. Over the same period the number of children achieving Level 5 has risen too, by 12 percentage points in English to 29 per cent and 7 percentage points in mathematics to 24 per cent.

3.5 The Literacy Hour and the daily mathematics lesson have succeeded because of the skill and enthusiasm of teachers and pupils. As a result, we remain on course for, and determined to achieve, the targets that, by 2002, 80 per cent of 11 year olds should have achieved Level 4 or above in English, and 75 per cent Level 4 or above in mathematics.

3.6 It is encouraging that variations in achievement between areas are narrowing. Critically, the fastest improving areas in the country are among the most disadvantaged. In 2000 the lowest scoring Local Education Authority in the English tests for 11 year olds achieved better than the national average of just four years ago. Moreover, the achievement differences between ethnic groups are beginning to be addressed. Education Authorities with high ethnic minority populations are amongst the most rapidly improving in the country and in Education Action Zones, progress is faster than in the rest of the country.

3.7 There is evidence too that the strategies are benefiting children with Special Educational Needs. They have been welcomed by a range of bodies representing those with Special Educational Needs.

3.8 Underpinning this progress has been the commitment of governors and staff in schools, growing investment per pupil in primary education, the class size reductions at infant level and the provision of many more trained classroom assistants. Our homework guidelines, proposing moderate and sensible amounts of homework at this level have been widely welcomed. We have provided funding for an additional 23 million books across the school system, making a real impact on the quality of resources available in the classroom.

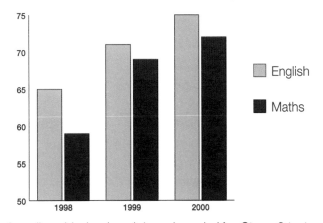

Percentage of pupils achieving Level 4 or above in Key Stage 2 tests

CLEEVE PRIMARY SCHOOL

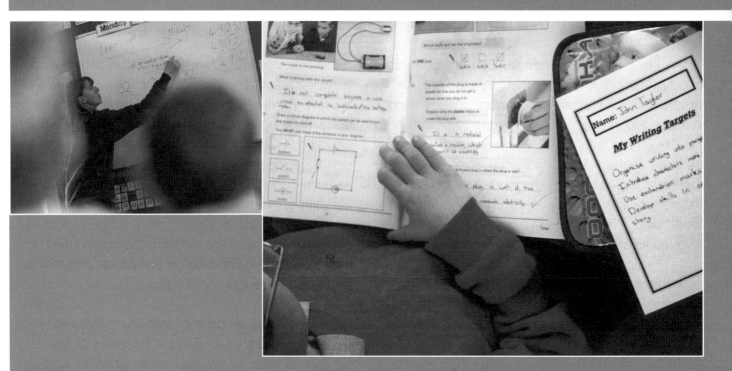

Cleeve is a mixed infant and junior community school, with 311 pupils and 52 nursery age pupils. The school serves the socio-economically deprived Noddle Hill area of the Bransholme Estate in Hull. The percentages of pupils eligible for free school meals, and with Special Educational Needs are well above the national average. Pupil mobility is high with significant numbers of children being admitted to the school in each year group.

Results for the school have risen dramatically this year: the percentage of 11 year old pupils reaching the expected level rose between 1999 and 2000 from 32 to 78 per cent in English, from 37 to 71 per cent in mathematics and from 78 to 98 per cent in science. Some of the keys to this success include:

Getting the basics right. The National Literacy and Numeracy Strategies have played a very significant part. These have been underpinned by the high-quality of teaching; the excellent behaviour of the children; comprehensive pastoral support; the contribution of support assistants in the classroom and around the school; and effective leadership by the management team.

A rigorous approach to self-evaluation. The school has a rigorous approach to self-evaluation and sets targets for each pupil. It is a member of the local Education Action Zone, which has created a climate for change by raising expectations and aspirations both within the school and amongst the wider community.

3.9 We are also providing additional support to small primary schools in particular. We have made available an additional £80 million a year through the Small Schools Administration Fund to enable small schools to purchase administrative support and so relieve teachers of burdens. We have encouraged schools to develop innovative approaches to sharing resources such as bursars, technicians and specialist teachers and increased co-operation between schools.

3.10 For example, two or more small schools, working together, can employ a bursar between them to carry out the administrative work of the schools. This approach can make a significant difference to reducing the workload of heads and other senior teachers in small schools. Horton Primary School (overleaf) demonstrates the use of Support Fund money.

...AND WE WILL ENSURE IT CONTINUES

3.11 Building on this progress, we can now go further and complete the transformation of primary education. To do so, we must address a number of important challenges. The five key ones are:
- Continuing to make progress in the basics, to the 2002 targets and beyond.
- Continuing to narrow inequalities in achievement through targeted support to those areas and groups of children who need most help.
- Continuing the drive to transform the pupil:adult ratio (average number of children per adult) in schools.
- Enriching the curriculum for every child.
- Strengthening the transition from primary to secondary school.

All children must have sound foundations in the basics

3.12 Achieving the 2002 targets for English and mathematics will represent a step-change to primary education, but we have never believed that would be the end of the story. Every child matters, so we want to ensure that every child is either on track to achieve at least Level 4 or receiving additional targeted support to help them towards that. We will never give up seeking to ensure that every child learns the '3 Rs' to the highest standards of which he or she is capable.

3.13 We will consult on targets for 2004 that 85 per cent of 11 year olds should achieve Level 4 or above in each of English and mathematics. And all children at whatever level should be making progress. Those who are capable of achieving more should be pushed to do so, which is why we also want to build on the already significant increases in the number of 11 year olds achieving Level 5. We will also consult on a target that at least 35 per cent of 11 year olds reach that level by 2004.

3.14 We intend to ensure that all children who fall behind their peers receive additional support either in small groups or, if necessary, one to one. We know that early intervention is the most effective; so we want to ensure that problems are identified early, and that support is then targeted to address them. We will ensure that children who have Special Educational Needs are identified quickly, but also that children who simply need some catch-up support do not have to go through a lengthy or bureaucratic process to receive it. We will promote better, more relevant and more comparable baseline assessment information at the end of the Foundation Stage, so that teachers have an accurate picture of what children can do at the start of their primary years. This will support the early identification of Special Educational Needs, and provision of catch-up support.

HORTON PRIMARY SCHOOL

Horton primary school has transformed its ICT provision by working with other local schools using money from the Small Schools Support Fund. The school, located in rural South Gloucestershire, has 46 pupils, one full-time teacher and two part-time teachers. It pooled money from the Support Fund with three other small local schools – Old Sodbury, Trinity School in Acton Turville, and Hawkesbury to employ a freelance ICT teacher.

Since September, the new teacher has used new networked computers bought with NGfL Funding to train groups of up to 16 children in the essentials of the new technology. Children from the 4 schools are taught together. With expert advice, the schools have already invested in an impressive range of software and equipment – including digital cameras, scanners and a CD writer. Now the school would like to develop videoconferencing facilities and make links with schools abroad.

3.15 We know that ICT can help schools to provide this more individualised learning and support. Research by the British Educational Communications and Technology Agency (BECTa) demonstrates that at Key Stage 2 the standards achieved at schools with good ICT provision are higher on average than at schools with poor ICT provision. Primary schools are embracing ICT: 86 per cent are connected to the Internet; on average there is now a computer for every 13 primary pupils. Increasingly, teachers see ICT as one of the key resources available to them in raising standards. The Horton and Priory case studies illustrate this.

3.16 We are determined that all ethnic minority pupils should secure results which are as good as those for other pupils. Many ethnic minority children have benefited from the recent rise in school standards, and children from some minority ethnic groups achieve highly. But for others, there is still an unacceptable inequality in levels of attainment which must be reduced. Through our analysis of the impact of our reforms we will enable schools to understand the reasons why some pupils make slower progress and encourage them to set high expectations for all. Where necessary we will provide the extra support that may be needed.

3.17 The integration into the National Literacy Strategy of the teaching of English as an additional language is already bringing substantial benefits. We will ensure that the emerging best practice in teaching children whose first language is not English is adopted across the whole curriculum. We will invest over £150 million a year for the next three years in raising the attainment of ethnic minority children with the aim of closing the differences that exist between the attainment of different groups.

3.18 Marion Richardson Primary School in Tower Hamlets shows what can be achieved. Some 400 of the 489 pupils in the school have English as a second language, and there are high proportions with Special Educational Needs and receiving free school meals. OFSTED recently described the school as demonstrating 'superb' racial harmony. All pupils have benefited from successful implementation of the National Literacy and Numeracy Strategies: the school's Key Stage 2 results were amongst the best in the country. The school has strong support from parents and governors.

3.19 Other important gaps in achievement exist, including that between girls and boys in English. We are determined that our policies should progressively address these gaps. We will continue to challenge underperformance and disseminate good practice, including the effective pupil tracking systems which enable schools to monitor the progress of each pupil and target support accordingly. We will continue to promote high expectations and ensure that the curriculum includes and motivates all pupils. The Priory School case study on page 34 sets out an example of how some of these methods can transform a school.

We will continue to improve pupil: adult ratios

3.20 We promised that by 2002 infant class sizes would be reduced to 30 or fewer pupils. Already this has been achieved for 98 per cent of 5, 6 and 7 year olds and we are on course to meet the pledge ahead of schedule in September 2001, thanks to our investment of £620 million. Research has shown that class size makes most difference at this early age. Some 450,000 children are benefiting from classes of 30 or under as a result of our policy. And 176,000 more children are benefiting from being in classes of under 25.

3.21 As children get older and become more used to the disciplines of school, the size of their class or group becomes less critical, but high levels of personal contact with adults remain crucial throughout primary education. Good pupil: adult ratios in primary schools mean more personal attention to meet the needs of all children and the opportunity to provide targeted support to children who have Special Educational Needs, special talents or have fallen behind their peers in a specific aspect of the curriculum. We have supported greatly improved training for teaching assistants, who are increasingly professional and provide important support in these clearly-defined roles.

3.22 For these reasons, for older children in primary schools, we want to see extra staff and expertise available to enable schools to target support flexibly to meet the talents and aspirations of individuals. Different mixtures of teachers, support staff and technology can be used to teach different types of lesson. Headteachers in consultation with their staff and governors should be able to decide how staff should be deployed for the benefit of the children in the school.

3.23 As the figure on page 35 shows, we have improved the pupil:adult ratio over the last three years from 18.4 to 17.2 for infants and equally significantly for juniors – from 23.1 to 21.7. We expect to see continued year-on-year improvements in the national average pupil:adult ratio. We are investing £73 million to begin to spread the benefits of smaller classes to the junior years, and training and funding 20,000 additional teaching assistants to improve support in the classroom.

PRIORY SCHOOL

Priory School in Slough is an example of an institution that mixes innovation and new technologies with good teaching and strong parental support. The school has 786 pupils aged 3 to 12, including 25 per cent from ethnic minority groups and 25 per cent with Special Educational Needs.

Priory has led the way in embracing Information and Communications Technology (ICT) as both a tool to enhance effective teaching and learning and a further means by which to engage and interact with pupils.

Priory's effective use of ICT includes:
- multimedia whiteboard presentation aids in the classroom;
- use of electronic pencils by pupils;
- use of computer painting and image manipulation packages;
- word processing for all 8 year olds, and spreadsheet use by the age of 11.

The school recently received an outstanding OFSTED inspection report.

3.24 As additional adults are brought in to the classroom to carry out a variety of roles, pupil: adult ratios will become the best measure of the level of support and attention that older primary children receive. More trained teaching assistants will provide increased support for class teachers; and other trained professionals will provide increased catch-up support for children who fall behind. The Dalton Foljambe School case study on page 38 is an example of how assistants are helping to raise standards already.

All children should experience a broad curriculum

3.25 High achievement in the basic areas of reading, writing and mathematics unlocks achievement in other subjects; it is essential if children are to have access to a range of opportunities later in life; it opens new worlds to children; and is itself motivating and enjoyable. But it is not enough on its own.

3.26 Primary education must open up for children a broad curriculum and a wide range of experiences. We know that schools and parents rightly continue to see creativity, art, music and sport as important parts of school life. We want every pupil to have opportunities to achieve in these areas.

3.27 Sport and physical education are a vital part of schools' activities and we want to increase the amount that takes place in schools at all levels. Apart from contributing to the health of pupils, they can also encourage personal development, boost pupils' self-confidence and increase commitment and attendance.

3.28 The Government's ambition for sport in schools was set out in *A Sporting Future for All* in April 2000. Since then, we have announced several significant developments including a doubling of funding for the School Sport Co-ordinator programme, so that by 2004 there will be a network of 1,000 Co-ordinators in secondary schools ensuring high-quality PE and sporting opportunities. They will work with Specialist Sports Colleges and link with families of primary and secondary schools. About 5,000 primary schools will be involved. We have also made available £580 million from the New Opportunities Fund for sport in and around schools and remain committed to the goal of increasing the amount of time that pupils spend on sport and other extra-curricular activities. This is why we recently announced our intention to offer an entitlement for school PE and sport so that any child who wanted would have access to 2 hours of high-quality sport or PE each week during and after-school. This is supported by the Healthy Schools Programme.

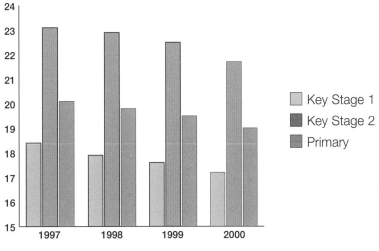

Pupil:adult ratios in primary schools

NEWDIGATE PRIMARY SCHOOL

Newdigate Primary School has shown what can be achieved through the commitment of staff in taking forward the national strategies. The school, of 276 pupils, came off special measures in November 1999 and has been one of top 10 improving schools over the last two years. A number of strategies have contributed to the school's success.

Children have targets in their books so they know what level they are working on and what they need to do to achieve the next level. In writing, Year 6 children are shown what Level 4/5 achievement looks like. Past papers are also used for comprehension skills – children mark their own papers and see the answer modelled, using an OHP, by the teacher.

The school has also used its data to pair boys in Year 4 and Year 6 on reading and spelling and has introduced an hour of independent writing per week from Year1 upwards. A weekly 'flexi-time' period for extra English and mathematics focuses on areas pupils find difficult.

Headteacher Rachael Waterfield says: "We are very open and honest with our children. We place a strong emphasis on setting clear targets for individual pupils."

3.29 Our investment in music has given a real boost to music in schools and to help talented young musicians. We have done much to support better teaching and learning of music. In 1999, we established the Music Standards Fund, designed to tackle the problem of decline in Local Education Authority music services, including facilities such as instrumental tuition and specialist teaching. Between 1999 and 2004, we will be investing £270 million through the Fund (£60 million a year by 2003–04), to protect existing services and allow their expansion.

3.30 We are also strengthening significantly our support for artistic, cultural and creative activities. We are supporting the Space for Sport and Arts programme which will create multipurpose sports and arts facilities in around 300 primary schools in some of the most deprived areas of the country. Furthermore, we have introduced a national strategy – Creative Partnerships – which will enable children to develop skills in, and understanding of, creativity, through an enhanced programme of artistic and creative opportunities. It will bring schools together with theatres, galleries and other providers of the arts and create sustainable partnerships between them. From April 2002, 15 new Creative Partnerships will be established in areas around the country where children will be most likely to benefit from the partnerships' services and activities, in areas of educational, socio-economic and cultural need.

3.31 Our innovative Museums and Galleries programme, launched in 1999, is supporting over 60 projects aimed at developing educational links between schools and museums and galleries. The projects cover a wide range of subjects, some with an ICT focus. They all provide examples of how children can experience new, exciting ways of learning about curriculum subjects through visits and working with professional educationalists employed in museums and galleries. We are evaluating the programme to learn lessons about how schools can build sustainable partnerships with local arts providers to enrich the styles of teaching that children are exposed to throughout the learning day.

3.32 Culture Online will also provide a new resource for schools. Culture Online will offer millions of children and their teachers the chance to interact online with artists, museums, galleries, theatres and digital creators to explore all aspects of British culture and heritage, and to develop their own creative skills in all aspects of arts, film and design. Culture Online will commission interactive material from cultural organisations and artists which support teaching and learning of the curriculum at all stages. Culture Online will start piloting at the end of 2001, and by 2004 would expect to be getting more hits from British school students than any other website worldwide.

DALTON FOLJAMBE SCHOOL

Dalton Foljambe School provides an example of how a primary school has used classroom assistants to develop all pupils' performance, particularly those with Special Educational Needs. Support staff have been crucial in increasing the individual attention that all pupils receive, helping both to identify and overcome difficulties. This is an important factor in the school's recent impressive performance in the key areas of English, mathematics and science.

Pupils experiencing difficulties are identified early and prompt provision is made by the school to resolve them. Teachers plan adapted work for pupils and support assistants, who have been trained to give additional literacy support sensitively. Pupils work in small groups or individually on programmes devised to meet their individual targets.

All pupils including those with behavioural difficulties, make very good progress towards their targets.

3.33 We also want to enable children in primary schools to get an early start in skills that will be important as they grow older such as Modern Foreign Languages. We have done a great deal to support Modern Foreign Languages teaching in primary schools. Around 20 per cent of primary schools already offer language learning in some form, which we aim to support and enhance. In September 1999 we began an Early Language Learning (Good Practice) Project. This Project has 18 pilots covering around 150 schools. An early years languages framework is now being developed, which may be built on to produce further Schemes of Work or other curriculum support and guidance.

3.34 We also intend, as a specific response to last year's Nuffield report on this issue, to make it easier for primary schools to access the language facilities of Specialist Language Colleges. The increase in the number of Specialist Language Colleges and the increased focus on their role as 'hubs' of excellence will provide access for primary schools to Modern Foreign Languages expertise and help to raise standards in the neighbourhoods around the Language Colleges.

3.35 We would also like, as resources permit, to see more primary schools, initially in areas of disadvantage, using more specialist teachers (who in some cases might be Advanced Skills Teachers) to provide lessons in music, art, drama and sports for example and to develop the skills of primary teachers in these areas, sharing specialist teachers between schools where that makes sense. Extending the use of these teachers will not only bring fresh expertise into schools, but also provide more time out of the classroom for class teachers to plan collaboratively and take part in professional development. We are particularly keen that we provide time to support the vital work of SEN Co-ordinators (SENCOs). We will examine effective and innovative approaches to deploying staff and making best use of their time and disseminate best and innovative practice around the system.

3.36 The Government is also determined that children should have greater access to extra-curricular activities and after-school clubs. Already, 97 per cent of schools provide some support of this sort and 7 out of 10 schools increased their provision between 1998 and 2000. We intend to move further, so that in time, every child at primary school who wants to has the opportunity to learn a musical instrument and try one of a range of sports. To make this possible we will expand the availability of out-of-school learning opportunities and continue to invest in school music at the new higher levels.

We will provide support to help children to overcome social problems

3.37 A range of social problems can prevent children achieving their potential. The Government has introduced policies to tackle social exclusion and to eradicate child poverty. As part of this, we have established the Children's Fund to support services which will identify children and young people who are showing early signs of disturbance and provide them and their families with the support they need to get back on track. Its aim is to prevent children falling into drug abuse, truancy, exclusion, unemployment and crime.

3.38 The Fund will provide £450 million over three years, of which £380 million will be targeted at preventive work for children aged 5–13. The Fund will help vulnerable children and young people particularly by helping them before a crisis. The Fund will pay for services such as mentoring programmes, parenting education and support, counselling and advice. The remaining £70 million will be for a local network of Children's Funds to be administered by the voluntary sector, for children of all ages, and will focus on helping local and community groups to provide local solutions to the problem of child poverty. It will include a strong emphasis on children's and young people's own aspirations and views.

3.39 The Children's Fund will play an important part in ensuring that schools are able to concentrate effectively on their key task of raising standards for all children. In the past, children who have experienced problems have often slipped into truancy or exclusion, and into a downward spiral from which it can be difficult to escape. In seeking to support children likely to face a crisis, and in helping to break the cycle of poverty and disadvantage, the Children's Fund will seek to head off some of the most difficult problems that children and, by extension, schools face.

3.40 We are working with the families of primary schoolchildren, to support parents and to raise awareness of the importance of home support for schools. We will also look to promote Family Focused Schools in areas of high disadvantage, providing childcare, study and family support, using schools as a community resource. Such schools could:

- Provide a longer, more flexible day through a variety of forms of childcare.
- Provide support for parents by, for example, making parenting classes available.
- Ensure that parents are involved in identifying the services they need, including for example healthcare and social services.
- Be sponsored by local employers as a way of encouraging a greater contribution from them to childcare.

There are already good examples of such schools in the system. We intend to draw out and build on that good practice.

WE WILL IMPROVE THE TRANSITION TO SECONDARY SCHOOL

3.41 Transitions between different institutions and phases of education are always important. It is critical that, although children may move school, they do not experience a break in their education, or 'mark time' as schools work out the level they are working at. From the Sure Start programme in the earliest years, through early years education and the better integration of baseline assessment in the first years of primary school, the Government is paying particular attention to making sure that transitions are made as smoothly and effectively as possible.

3.42 For many years transition from primary to secondary school has been inadequate. Far too many 11 year olds have lost momentum in the last few weeks of primary school and over the summer holiday before they start secondary school. All too often when they do start secondary school, teachers start with 'a clean slate' and set expectations lower than they should be. The result has been that by the end of the first year in secondary school many pupils have made little progress and lost motivation and as many as 30 per cent actually achieve lower standards than in the last year of primary school. Both primary and secondary teachers acknowledge that this state of affairs is unacceptable. The step-change in the performance of primary schools in recent years has added to the overwhelming view that action is needed. We have therefore begun to address what, for the last generation or more, has been neglected or swept aside as an intractable problem.

3.43 Already we have:

- Introduced a common transfer form for pupil performance data and other information, which can be used electronically, and which reduces bureaucracy as well as improving the transfer for pupils.
- Provided 2,500 summer schools for 75,000 11 year olds each year.
- Developed 'transition modules' in English and mathematics for teachers to use in the last term of primary school and the first year of secondary, which enable continuity and progression for pupils as they transfer.
- Enabled thousands of secondary teachers to watch skilled primary colleagues teaching literacy hours and daily mathematics lessons, thus raising expectations of 11 year olds and strengthening professional relationships.
- Piloted in Education Action Zones a number of ideas for improved collaboration between primary and secondary schools. Schools in many zones share both staff and premises, run peer mentoring programmes across the phases and link up more closely to plan and try out new ideas. In Newham, for example, a 'virtual learning space' gives zone schools common access to curriculum materials and best practice via an EAZ Intranet.

3.44 There are many models of good practice from which we can learn. For example, The Archbishop Blanch Church of England School in Liverpool works with local primary schools to develop cross-phase projects, which aid transition. These include joint curriculum schemes, interactive learning for literacy and numeracy, portfolios of examples of work in subjects taught in both phases and masterclasses delivered to exceptionally able primary children.

3.45 In the future we plan to develop this work and to make further improvements including:

- Ensuring better use of the second half of the last summer term at primary school, by providing training in the use of transition and encouraging secondary schools to receive some or all of their new pupils for two or three weeks in advance of the summer break.
- More extensive provision of summer schools so that ultimately there would be summer school provision at every secondary school.
- Teaching frameworks and materials that cross the divide. These are already available in English and mathematics: the frameworks which have been such a crucial part of the primary strategies have now been extended to cross the transition and include Years 7, 8 and 9. Meanwhile nationally produced Schemes of Work, which have proved immensely popular with teachers, are available in every National Curriculum subject for ages 7–11 and 11–14.
- Joint training for primary and secondary teachers.
- Introducing the new 'Common Basic Data Set' by 2002, which will enable schools and the system to track each individual pupil's progress effectively even when they change schools, and will reduce bureaucracy for schools.
- Raising expectations and better catch-up arrangements for those who need them between the ages of 11 and 14 (see the next chapter).
- Providing better advice and support to parents so that they can play their part in their child's transition from primary to secondary school.

3.46 With these building blocks in place, children will be better prepared than ever before for secondary education. The loss of pace and progression, which has characterised the transfer from primary to secondary school for so long, can become a thing of the past.

CHAPTER 4
TRANSFORMING SECONDARY EDUCATION

FOR SECONDARY EDUCATION, OUR GOALS ARE HIGHER STANDARDS, MORE SCHOOL AUTONOMY AND DIVERSITY, AND MORE SUITABLE AND CHALLENGING PATHWAYS FOR PUPILS BEYOND 14.

We will:

- significantly enhance the diversity of secondary education, with every school having a distinctive mission and ethos and contributing to the community or to the wider education system;
- ensure a step change in performance in the early secondary years, including demanding targets for achievement in national tests at age 14;
- from age 13 or 14, ensure that the education system focuses far more than in the past on the individual talents and aspirations of pupils, with more early entries for GCSE and much greater choice of vocational and work-based routes;
- significantly increase the support available to schools in the most challenging circumstances, on condition that they sign up to demanding performance targets;
- narrow significantly the achievement gaps that exist by ethnic group, geographical area and gender, so that the education system delivers real equality of opportunity; and
- promote 'education with character' that stresses not just a broad curriculum but also opportunities for pupils to become active citizens of their school and community, and to develop all their talents including in sports and the arts.

4.1 In the 21st century, it will not be acceptable for young people to leave formal education with few skills. Everyone will need to be knowledgeable, to be able to reason, to think logically and creatively and to continue to learn throughout their lives. Only with this grounding will they be prepared for the fast-changing society and employment opportunities ahead. The Literacy and Numeracy Strategies in primary schools have begun the process of ensuring that everyone can read, write and add up. The National Grid for Learning programme has done the same for the use of information technology. We need to ensure that we build on, rather than lose, this momentum when children enter their secondary phase of education. This will require much higher expectations of all, greater diversity of provision and secondary education much more closely tailored to the talents of individuals.

4.2 We want to make current best practice the norm, and we want some schools to go beyond this, so that the best schools provide a leading edge.

WE HAVE MADE PROGRESS...

4.3 The framework for continuous improvement, described in Chapter 1, has enabled many secondary schools to improve steadily in recent years. More young people are achieving high standards at age 16 and 18 than ever before. Fewer than ever are leaving school without qualifications: 33,000 in 2000, down from 45,000 in 1997.

4.4 Policies have been put in place to enhance progress at secondary level in the most challenging areas. The Excellence in Cities programme, described on page 45, will involve 1,000 secondary schools in urban areas by September 2001. New funding has been allocated to enable over 500 secondary schools with the lowest attainment to develop plans to meet ambitious minimum performance targets for 2004 and 2006.

4.5 Progress has also been made in giving more secondary schools a distinct identity. The number of specialist schools with specialisms in technology, the arts, sport and modern foreign languages has been rapidly increased to around 600. In addition just two years after the start of the programme there are already 182 secondary Beacon schools. By September 2001, there will be 1000 Beacons, including some 250 at secondary level.

4.6 Above all, secondary schools have benefited from increased funding over the last four years, and from taking increased control of their own destiny. On average, schools will have some £700 more per pupil in 2003–04 than in 1997–98. Similarly, tripling the capital investment, including significant amounts devolved to schools themselves, has led to real improvements in the quality of many school buildings. Schools are benefiting from increased autonomy, and are innovating in a variety of ways, including by using time more flexibly and through the use of ICT (see the Excellence in Cities model).

4.7 As at primary level, we have emerging evidence that schools are narrowing the achievement gap between boys and girls and enabling all pupils, irrespective of ethnic background to achieve more. The most recent GCSE data shows that the children of unskilled manual workers have made the fastest progress of any social class – with a 10 per cent improvement between 1997 and 1999, from 20 percent to 30 per cent, in the numbers achieving 5 or more A*– C grade GCSEs. Furthermore, the achievement of some minority ethnic groups improved much more rapidly than the national average over the same period.

George Spencer's success is based on a mixture of innovation, willingness to utilise the potential of ICT and the dedicated commitment of its staff. Its average GCSE score is amongst the highest in Nottinghamshire.

The school's Technology College status has helped it to pioneer a 'virtual learning community'. Its whole-school, industry-standard computer network allows staff, parents and students to access the school intranet 24 hours a day, 7 days a week. Curriculum and learning materials and all work files can be accessed remotely, ensuring maximum flexibility to meet learners' needs on demand. As a Beacon school, George Spencer is developing distance learning packages which will be accessible to staff in other schools.

As a Training School providing initial teacher training, George Spencer demonstrates and develops excellent teacher training practice. The school has employed many adults who provide learning support to students while training for Qualified Teacher Status and it also recruits adult learning support for other schools in the region.

... BUT TRANSFORMATION IS NOW THE TASK

4.8 The central task in the next five years is to bring about that transformation with higher standards and greater equality of opportunity. We want to enable all schools to develop three key characteristics of successful secondary schools: effective leadership; a resolute focus on raising standards throughout the school; and a strong ethos. Successful schools are proud of their distinctive identity and passionate about their mission. Many secondary schools exhibit these characteristics already. A key step to replicating these characteristics across the system is the sustained implementation of the Excellence in Cities programme. In addition it will require the following major developments:

- A major extension of diversity in the secondary school system, and a variety of new approaches to encouraging each school to develop its own distinctive mission and ethos, including further expansion of the specialist schools programme.
- A continued increase in schools' autonomy, particularly where they are successful.
- A concerted drive to improve the quality of teaching and raise standards in the first three years of secondary school.
- The development of a new choice of flexible pathways for 13/14–19 year olds to enable much greater tailoring of education to the talents and aspirations of individuals.
- Further substantial improvements in achievement at schools in the most challenging circumstances.
- A new emphasis on enrichment, offering all pupils not just a broad curriculum but also opportunities to develop all their talents, become active citizens of their school and community and benefit from outdoor adventure activity.

EXTENDING DIVERSITY

4.9 The individual school taking responsibility for improving its performance is the key to higher standards. Success results from good leadership, good teaching, clear goals and supportive partnerships. We have progressively given all schools greater control over their own future by removing constraints and providing greatly increased resources. The premise of our policy is intervention in inverse proportion to success. We have encouraged successful secondary schools to make the most of the increasing levels of delegated funding to innovate and to develop and spread best practice.

4.10 Schools are now responsible for their own performance, for the conduct of the school and its discipline, for the control of school premises, the repair and maintenance of buildings and, in the case of foundation and voluntary aided schools, for admissions. We have also helped to ensure that governors, heads and teachers have the right support, from reformed Education Authorities and from elsewhere, to do their jobs as effectively as they can. All schools now enjoy many of the freedoms that were formerly only available to the grant-maintained sector. The 1998 legislation gives schools greater choice about their category, and permits any community school that wishes, with local agreement, to propose transfer from community to foundation status.

4.11 One of the benefits of giving schools this freedom to deploy their own resources, while holding them accountable for their performance in raising standards, is that it enables schools to develop their own character. The evidence suggests that schools with a strong sense of identity or ethos perform best.

THE EXCELLENCE IN CITIES MODEL

Excellence in Cities (EiC) is designed to tackle underachievement in some of the country's most challenging areas. It was launched in March 1999, and by September 2001, will cover around a third of all secondary age pupils in 1,000 schools. From September 2001, for the first time, the approach adopted in the programme will be introduced in smaller areas of deprivation beyond the big cities, through new Excellence Clusters.

EiC aims to raise standards and at the same time to give parents renewed confidence that their children will receive a high-quality education wherever they go to school. It is based on the principles that there should be high expectations of all pupils, whatever their background; that there should be greater diversity beyond the basic National Curriculum; that schools achieve more when they work together to raise standards; and that we need to extend learning opportunities for pupils of all abilities, building on the talents and aspirations of each one.

Through the programme additional resources are provided to:
• extend opportunities for Gifted and Talented pupils by providing focused programmes within schools and university summer school places;
• provide access to Learning Mentors who help pupils to overcome barriers to learning outside the school and free teachers to teach;
• put in place Learning Support Units to tackle disruption alongside improved provision for excluded pupils;
• increase the numbers of Beacon and specialist schools in city areas;
• introduce new City Learning Centres with state of the art ICT; and
• establish small Education Action Zones to raise performance in small clusters of schools.

The success of EiC is underpinned by strong partnerships between all secondary schools and their Local Education Authority. The schools work together for the benefit of the whole community. There is no bidding involved. Resources go where they are most needed. The approach has been widely welcomed by schools and teachers.

The programme is still in its infancy but already, schools in EiC areas have shown faster improvement than schools elsewhere, both in terms of the proportion of pupils achieving 5 or more A*– C grade GCSEs and those getting at least one GCSE. Encouragingly, improvements have been fastest in the most deprived schools.

THOMAS TELFORD

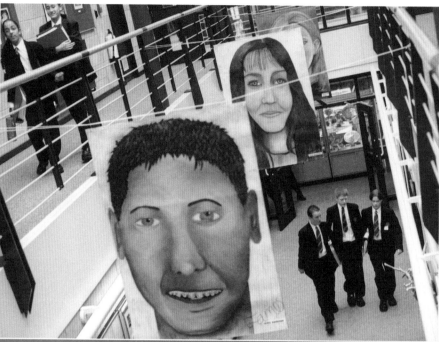

Thomas Telford School's outstanding examination result success can be explained by a number of key factors.

High standards are expected from students and all achievements are recognised and celebrated. Pupils set their own targets with guidance from teachers. There are ten reports to parents during the year and there is a very high level of parental participation. Bullying is not tolerated. The school has a balanced intake from across a wide area.

ICT pervades the school. It has more than 20 interactive whiteboards, all linked to the Internet. The videoconferencing facility can link to a number of other schools including five local primary schools who are partners under the Beacon schools programme. The school has created an interactive online 'live' curriculum. This allows students and their parents to access the school curriculum from any computer with an Internet connection.

The longer school day, developed by the staff of the school, embraces the imaginative use of technology, and innovative use of time, coupled with proven traditional teaching methods. Over 150 pupils a year play sport in district, county and regional teams.

Kevin Satchwell, headteacher, said, "Everyone involved with this school knows what is expected of them and enjoys being part of a very successful team."

4.12 Furthermore, greater diversity of provision means that schools will be creating a wider array of innovative practice, which can be spread to the whole family of schools. As a result, the system as a whole will become more capable of meeting the different talents and aspirations of individuals. For these reasons we want to encourage all secondary schools to develop a distinctive mission and ethos. Of course, we want to foster schools' initiative and provide support, not to impose on the leadership, management and staff of a school particular characteristics or non-teaching requirements which they do not believe they are capable of managing. For this reason, our approach at secondary level is different from that at primary, where small schools often do not have the capacity to take on additional administrative tasks.

4.13 Every school must be highly effective in teaching the main subjects of the National Curriculum. Our strategy for lower secondary and other changes will ensure that this is achieved for those currently underachieving (see paragraph 4.27). But we also want every school to develop its strengths and make a contribution beyond. In some cases this contribution will be as a faith school; in other cases it will be as a specialist school or Beacon school or a training school. Others will contribute through participation in an Education Action Zone or an Excellence in Cities partnership. Some schools may take on more than one of these roles. The important point is that every school should have the opportunity and responsibility to make a contribution to a family of schools, to the development of the system as a whole or to the local community. As the inspection system evolves, we would want to see it examining the way that each school plays its wider role as well as carrying out its core function.

4.14 In order to realise this vision of every school making a wider contribution, we will increase the number of ways that schools can do so. Specialist and Beacon schools are already funded for their responsibility to develop and spread best practice. We will enable more schools to achieve specialist or Beacon status. We have already announced that we will increase the number of specialist schools to 1,000 by 2004. We now want to accelerate that target, so that there will be 1,000 by 2003. In addition, we will lift the current restriction on the number of specialist schools in Education Authorities where there is already a high proportion. This will mean that schools wanting to take on a specialism will not be restricted just because other nearby schools already have a specialism. By 2006, we will seek to increase the number of specialist schools further, to 1,500, considerably more than double the number at present, and eight times the number in 1997.

4.15 As well as increasing the number of schools that can make a wider contribution through developing a specialism, we will also broaden the range of specialisms available. In addition to technology, languages, sport and the arts, we will offer schools three new specialist options: engineering; science; and business and enterprise. Business and enterprise schools will be expected to develop strong curriculum-business links and develop teaching strengths in business studies, financial literacy and enterprise-related vocational programmes. Widening the options in this way will mean that schools will spread good practice and promote innovation through the system in more subjects. They will be assisted by the Technology Colleges Trust broad bandwidth Intranet.

4.16 It is also critical that the system has a 'leading edge' of schools with a mission to promote innovative practice and exemplify the school of the future. We will, therefore, introduce in due course a new category of advanced specialist school which would be open to high-performing schools after five years in the specialist schools programme. They could volunteer to take on a number of innovative ideas from a 'menu' developed centrally in dialogue with existing, successful, specialist schools. In return they would receive an additional capital investment to strengthen their centre of excellence. The 'menu' might include such items as experimentation with distance learning or the preparation of high-quality curriculum materials. An important part of the advanced specialist role might also be initial teacher training, with many of the schools taking a leading role as training schools. Alternatively, some might contain a centre for leadership and management training in association with the National College for School Leadership.

4.17 In addition, we will expand the number of secondary Beacon schools. By September 2001 there will be 1,000 Beacon schools, including some 250 at secondary level. We will seek to expand the number at secondary level to 400 in the longer term. We will also designate some schools as Beacons that achieve particular effectiveness in teaching the skills relevant to the emerging economy, including promoting creativity and the use of ICT. And we will offer Beacon status to some schools that demonstrate excellence in working with their community. This would enable the many schools, which have an excellent record of working with parents and the wider community, to promote their successful practice.

4.18 We have increased the number and variety of schools within the state system supported by the churches and other major faith groups. Some 560 secondary schools are now provided by the Church of England or the Catholic Church. For the first time, Muslim, Sikh and Greek Orthodox schools have been brought inside the state system, and are being funded on the same basis as, for example, Church of England and Catholic schools have been for some time. We have also increased the number of Jewish schools. And we have indicated that we are ready to discuss with other community or privately-run schools the conditions on which they might enter the publicly-provided sector.

4.19 Schools supported by the churches and other major faith groups are, of course, valued by members of those groups. They also have a good record of delivering a high-quality of education to their pupils and many parents welcome the clear ethos of these schools. We therefore wish to welcome more schools provided by the churches and other major faith groups and by other voluntary and community groups, where there is clear local demand from parents and the community. We are pleased, for example, to see that Lord Dearing's report to the Archbishops' Council recommends that the Church of England increase the number of secondary schools that it supports, particularly in areas where there are few or no Anglican schools. We know other faith communities are also interested in extending their contribution to education. We intend to change the capital funding arrangements to make them more favourable to enable this to occur (see Chapter 6). The new school sponsorship proposals set out in paragraph 4.23 will also be of interest to faith groups and schools seeking to acquire faith sponsors.

4.20 The City Academy programme, launched last April, enables sponsors from the private and voluntary sectors to establish new schools whose running costs are fully met by the state. City Academies offer a radical option to help raise achievement in areas of historic underperformance by bringing a new and distinctive approach to school management and governance. We will expand the programme and, in future, will welcome proposals from those who want to establish all-through (age 5–18) schools as well as secondary schools.

4.21 City Academies are all-ability schools with the capacity to transform the education of children in areas of disadvantage and need. They will raise standards by innovative approaches to management, governance, teaching and the curriculum, offering a broad and balanced curriculum with a specialist focus in one area. City Academies will involve major investment for refurbishment, ICT and learning resources.

4.22 Six City Academy working partnerships have so far been announced in Brent, Haringey, Hillingdon, Lambeth, Liverpool and Middlesbrough. Sponsors from the voluntary and private sectors, Church and other faith groups are involved as sponsors. We will be announcing more Academies shortly. We intend to extend the programme year on year and welcome proposals from sponsors and interested local partners.

4.23 In addition, we intend to develop a new model which would enable an external private or voluntary sector sponsor to take responsibility for a weak or failing school against a fixed-term contract of, say, five to seven years with renewal subject to performance. This would create a new way for private and voluntary sponsors or existing successful schools to support the management of weak or failing schools. This will further develop the model used at King's Manor, Guildford, where '3Es', a charitable foundation from The City Technology College, Kingshurst, was responsible for establishing the new school (Kings College) and is currently supporting its management and development for a period of ten years. It also builds on the successful experience of specialist schools, where a formal assessment of management quality, and performance targets and review, are integral to the process of gaining and retaining specialist status.

4.24 This option will also enable successful schools to work in partnership with sponsors from the private and voluntary sectors, including recognised faith groups. Such a change might be attractive to schools embarking on a radical improvement strategy or seeking to develop a more distinct identity. Schools operating within this framework would remain subject to national policies on admissions and Special Educational Needs, and to local procedures for SEN, determining admissions arrangements and planning new places.

WE WILL OFFER GREATER AUTONOMY TO SUCCESSFUL SCHOOLS

4.25 Taken together, this range of opportunities will enable every secondary school to have a distinct mission, ethos and contribution to make to the system as a whole. We also want to ensure that, whatever their mission and ethos, schools that are demonstrably successful earn greater autonomy.

4.26 We have already changed the inspection arrangements so that successful schools receive a 'short' or light-touch inspection which places much greater emphasis on school self-evaluation. The early evidence suggests that this approach is working extremely well. We want now to extend their autonomy by offering greater freedom over the curriculum and over pay and conditions, as we did for Education Action Zones in the 1998 legislation. It will be entirely a matter for the schools concerned to decide whether to take advantage of the greater flexibility. The strong message we want to convey is that successful schools should, increasingly, be able to manage their own affairs. Minimum national standards will be respected. Schools need to have demonstrated continuous improvement or sustained excellence.

RAISING STANDARDS FOR 11–14 YEAR OLDS (KEY STAGE 3)

4.27 Standards for pupils aged 11–14 are not high enough. Teaching has generally been of lesser quality for this age group. Expectations have been too low. Pupils make far too little progress during these years. Attitudinal surveys show motivation falling and disaffection rising. It is at this age that for many pupils, especially boys, the roots of later failure are established. These problems are not confined to the English education system but the success of our National Literacy and Numeracy Strategies at primary level and the improvements we are making in transition arrangements, added to steadily increased funding, make us exceptionally well-placed to solve them. Only if we do, will we be able to see a step change in performance across the system not only at 14 but also 16, 18 and beyond. The evidence shows that level of attainment at 14 is a key determinant of GCSE performance: 93 per cent of those at Level 6 and 52 per cent of those at Level 5 go on to achieve 5 or more A*– C GCSEs at 16, but only 9 per cent of those at Level 4 do so.

4.28 Key components of the success of our National Strategies at primary level were high-quality professional development for teachers and stretching targets, focused on pupils' results. We intend to set ambitious targets in English, mathematics, science and ICT for 14 year olds in 2007 with milestone targets for 2004. We intend to announce the outcome of our consultation shortly.

4.29 The goals of our Key Stage 3 strategy are to ensure that by age 14, the vast majority of pupils have:
- Reached acceptable standards (Level 5 or above in the National Curriculum) in the basics of English, mathematics and science.
- Benefited from a broad curriculum, including learning each of the National Curriculum subjects.
- Learnt how to reason, to think logically and creatively and to take increasing responsibility for their own learning.

4.30 We also want to ensure that those who fall behind their peers in English and mathematics benefit from extra support through catch-up classes.

4.31 Increasingly after age 14 students will have greater choice among a variety of pathways to high standards. We therefore also want pupils to reach that age ready to make some important (though by no means irrevocable) choices.

4.32 Our pilot programme in 205 secondary schools in 17 different Local Education Authorities began last September. It builds on the success in recent years at primary level, on the improved transition arrangements and particularly on best practice in existing secondary schools. The early feedback from the pilot is encouraging. From September 2001 we intend to implement nationally a Key Stage 3 strategy as rigorous as the primary strategies have been, but taking account of the greater complexity of secondary schools and the secondary curriculum. We are already committing £82 million to support the new strategy next year and will shortly be announcing additional funding for implementation in future.

It will:
- Include annual targets for schools and Local Education Authorities for the performance of 14 year olds in English, mathematics and science, set in the context of the national targets.
- Extend the primary strategies for English and mathematics into lower secondary education, ensuring excellent materials and extra targeted support for those pupils and schools which have furthest to go to meet the targets.
- Strengthen the skills of all secondary teachers of English and mathematics, especially heads of department.
- Provide similar support for heads of science and science teachers.
- Enable all teachers, whatever their subjects, to support the teaching of literacy and numeracy.
- Promote ICT skills and the achievement of the new national ICT targets.
- Offer support to all teachers of all subjects to improve their skills in assessing pupils' work, setting individual targets for pupils and teaching reasoning and logical and creative thinking through their subject.
- Enable pupils whose first language is not English to take full advantage of teaching across the whole curriculum.

4.33 As part of this strategy we want to see all pupils stretched so that they achieve their full potential. This is as important for those with Special Educational Needs as for the most able. We want to see further increases in the extent of setting within subjects including express sets to enable those who are capable of doing so to advance beyond the levels set for their age and to take Key Stage 3 tests early. Those who are not making sufficient progress will get extra help and assistance. We intend over time to expand the existing summer school programmes so that, if necessary, pupils can get extra help before moving up to the next school year and so that extra opportunities can be offered to the most able.

4.34 For pupils with Special Educational Needs, we will adopt similar approaches. We need to have high expectations of these pupils, to tailor the curriculum to their needs and to ensure that teaching challenges and stretches them. We will build on our new framework, to ensure that children's needs are identified, assessed and met effectively. Critically, we will seek to ensure that problems are spotted quickly so that, for example, children with emotional and behavioural difficulties are helped as far as possible before they significantly disrupt the education of others. ICT can play a significant role in enhancing the educational opportunities for many children with learning disabilities, and we will look at a range of innovative approaches to promoting its use, including making technology available for pupils to use at home.

4.35 We intend to establish a new Centre for Gifted and Talented Youth, which will promote provision for gifted children in schools and establish intensive summer schools along the lines of those pioneered by Johns Hopkins University in Baltimore, USA. Its first task will be to pilot university-based summer schools for young people with exceptional talent in one or more subject areas.

4.36 The new World Class Tests which will be nationally available from next year in mathematics and problem-solving will ensure that gifted students can test themselves against the best anywhere in the world. We are working with other governments in, for example, Australia, the USA and Singapore in developing these tests.

The longer term for Key Stage 3

4.37 We expect these plans for the next three years to bring substantial progress. Beyond 2004 we may wish to consider shortening the current three-year key stage for 11–14 year olds to two years. If doing this contributed to tackling the perceived lack of pace and so increased motivation and engagement, then there would be potential for significant gains in pupil performance. We will pilot that idea over the next three years with a representative group of schools.

4.38 By 2004 the pupils transferring to secondary school will have had a full primary education since the introduction in 1998 of the National Literacy and Numeracy Strategies. At that point, we would therefore be in a position to extend nationally the shortened Key Stage 3, if the pilots had proved successful. However, we recognise that this would be a major change, and would want to consult fully with teachers and others before any decision to proceed. If this decision were taken, then we would provide sufficient time and support to enable it to be implemented effectively.

4.39 If pupils did complete Key Stage 3 a year earlier some could then make accelerated progress to GCSE or equivalent level, taking their exams a year ahead of the current schedule. Others would be able to take longer to complete GCSE, vocational GCSE or work-based courses and so achieve higher standards than they otherwise would. Clearly, if we were to make these radical changes we would need to examine the implications for the curriculum, the organisation of schools and for national, local and school level targets. These issues can be explored through the proposed pilot and will need to be widely discussed.

WE WILL INTRODUCE NEW PATHWAYS FOR 14 – 19 YEAR OLDS

4.40 As the quality and standards of learning in the lower secondary years improve, so young people will emerge at age 14 with a broad educational base of knowledge and understanding as well as advanced skills in the basics. They will also have developed the reasoning capacity and self-management which will enable them, with their teachers and personal advisers, to pursue a learning programme which reflects their own talents and aspirations. The more able will have the opportunity to proceed at a faster pace to GCSEs and beyond. We would expect many more to be making accelerated progress than is currently the case.

THE CENTRE FOR TALENTED YOUTH, JOHNS HOPKINS UNIVERSITY

4.41 From 14, the curriculum will offer a significant degree of choice. Every pupil will still take GCSEs, but increasingly they will be able to mix academic and vocational GCSEs and work-based options. A variety of opportunities will be tailored to each person's aptitudes, abilities and preferences, but all will demand high standards. The culture of leaving education for good at 16 will cease. GCSEs will be a progress check for most at the midpoint of the 14–19 programme. Increasingly, GCSEs will be taken at the end of Year 10 or in the autumn of Year 11 as well as the summer, enabling those who are ready, to move on to advanced level study early.

4.42 The individual pathways chosen at 14 will provide a broad programme and each will prepare young people for the world of work and for further study. There will be no compromise on standards – individual choice will be between high-quality routes providing high-quality education. And each route will offer a broad curriculum that prepares young people for an active and fulfiling adult life, whether at work, home or in the community. We will also be encouraging students to mix and match – to take vocational and academic GCSEs, but also to take GCSEs with work-based experience. We aim to break down the historic antagonism to vocational education as a route to success.

4.43 We intend to increase the percentage of pupils obtaining 5 or more GCSEs at grades A*– C (or equivalent).

By 2004, we will:
- Increase the proportion achieving the standard by 4 percentage points between 2002 and 2004.
- Ensure that at least 38 per cent achieve the standard in every Local Education Authority.

The Centre for Talented Youth at Johns Hopkins University was founded in 1979 to provide rigorous programmes to challenge very able students from 13 upwards. It uses an international talent search to identify those who will benefit most from what it can provide, and offers highly individualised programmes taught by top professionals in three-week summer programmes on teaching university campuses each year.

The aim is not to provide a curriculum which is radically different from that studied elsewhere, but rather to vary the pace and level of instruction. It also offers a range of subjects going well beyond what schools are able to provide, including paleobiology, geopolitics, astronomy and logic.

Starting on a small-scale in 1979, the Centre now runs programmes for more than 10,000 children each year across the United States, and approximately 100,000 young people apply annually for the Talent Search which affords entrance to the academic programmes.

We are developing new high-quality pathways for learning...

4.44 Young people will be able to study vocational and technical education as part of the normal school programme. High standard vocational options will be available to students across the ability range – those who excel at mathematics and the sciences, for example, will often want to study specialist engineering or design and technology options. But those young people who want a future career based on technical skills will be able to choose predominantly vocational programmes of study from age 14. We will strengthen and clarify the vocational options available in the later years of secondary education to enable this to happen. In particular, we will consult on the scope for increasing the time available for vocational study within the statutory framework of the National Curriculum, and in particular work-based options for craft and vocational study leading to an apprenticeship option.

4.45 This will not be a formula for determining a young person's future irrevocably at age 14. The pathways available will be flexible, allowing young people to mix academic and vocational study and switch between options as new abilities and interests become apparent. Whether students choose academic, vocational or a mixture of options at 14, a clear ladder of progression will be available to them at 16 in sixth forms, in colleges and in the workplace. Whatever their programmes of study – A levels, vocational A levels, a combination of these, or a Modern Apprenticeship – they will be able to pursue their studies to degree level if they reach the entrance standard for university. Foundation Degrees are being developed for those looking for a two-year programme with a strong vocational focus.

4.46 In the future, a 14 year old who wants to pursue a career in the hotel and catering industry may choose a Hospitality and Catering GCSE in a wider programme involving practical activity in the workplace and vocational study at a nearby college. Mathematics and science options would then have real practical value in relation to vocational study. At 16, after achieving GCSE mathematics and English, together with vocational GCSEs, he or she might take vocational A levels in Hospitality and Catering, Business, and Information and Communications Technology, leading to a Foundation Degree in Hotel Management. Equally, a 16 year old who has taken traditional GCSEs may go on to take vocational A levels or become employed as a Modern Apprentice, making progress in learning from the workplace and at college.

4.47 Directly, work-related learning will also be a valuable option for many 14–16 year olds. Progression routes into Foundation, and then Advanced, Modern Apprenticeships in skilled occupations will be routed back into work-related learning and placements for 14–16 year olds – giving confidence to young people to further develop their skills after leaving school. Qualifications towards apprenticeships could be gained while the young person was still at school – accelerating their learning progression. For example, a young person might study for an engineering GCSE alongside an NVQ in a specific occupation which they could then enter as a Foundation Modern Apprentice. Work placements would be arranged with local companies offering apprenticeship places. Evaluation work shows clearly that, when placements are of good quality and meet the aspirations of those undertaking them, standards of attainment rise, as do levels of attendance in school. We will expect all schools to offer work-related opportunities to their pupils, often in partnership with local colleges. All of these opportunities will need to be effectively tailored to students' needs.

4.48 As a consequence of these reforms, there will be hugely expanded opportunities for students to do part of their learning in colleges, the workplace and the community. Schools will remain at the heart of the learning process up to 16 (and in some cases beyond) but will need to rethink the role of teachers and mentors, who in some cases will spend some of the working week outside the school boundaries, teaching wherever the pupils are. Increasingly, schools, colleges and local businesses will work closely together to deliver these opportunities more effectively, and the students involved will be supported by a network of advisers and mentors including the Connexions Service.

4.49 Further Education colleges will have a major role in supporting our vision of more individual learning for 14–16 year olds. Schools and colleges will work in close partnership, drawing on their respective expertise, equipment and other resources. The approach may vary: pupils may spend considerable time in colleges or college staff may go to schools. In each case, learning can be effectively supported by the use of ICT and we will expect schools and colleges to build on existing good practice.

4.50 A secondary school with an emphasis on vocational pathways might establish close links with one of the Centres of Vocational Excellence currently being established in further education. Gifted and talented pupils at an 11–16 school could benefit from links with strong academic specialisms in the local sixth form college or centre, which itself would have a close relationship with higher education.

SECONDARY SCHOOLS IN CHALLENGING CIRCUMSTANCES

4.51 Extending diversity and encouraging dissemination of best practice will help all schools to improve. For schools in challenging circumstances, however, additional targeted support is vital if they are to enable their pupils to achieve high standards.

A great deal has already been done.
- The inspection process ensures that schools which are under-performing are identified and action taken to resolve their problems. The number of schools in special measures has fallen steadily and turn around times have been significantly reduced.
- Reformed Education Authorities are beginning to prevent failure as well as tackling it after it has occurred. The number of schools going into special measures was much lower in autumn 2000 than the previous autumn.
- Clear minimum performance targets for the lowest attaining secondary schools have been set: that by 2003 none should achieve fewer than 15 per cent of pupils getting 5 higher grades at GCSE; by 2004 none fewer than 20 per cent; and by 2006 none fewer than 25 per cent.

4.52 These targets are not set in a vacuum. Our policies will ensure that every secondary school with fewer than 25 per cent achieving 5 or more A*– Cs at GCSE or more than 35 per cent on free school meals receives extra targeted assistance and the opportunity, school by school and community by community, to improve performance.

We have introduced programmes to support schools facing problems...

4.53 Three programmes have already been designed and implemented to deal with underperformance across a geographical area.

- **73 Education Action Zones** have been established to promote innovation and higher standards in small pockets of deprivation, whether urban or rural. They normally involve two or three secondary schools and their feeder primary schools. There is growing evidence of their positive impact, especially so far on primary schools and on transition. As their programmes continue, we would expect to see improved performance feeding through at secondary level in the years ahead. We intend to encourage all EAZs to include early education within their scope, so that universal provision of early education for those whose parents want it is seen as the foundation for future learning and success.
- **Excellence in Cities** has been introduced in three phases (see Excellence in Cities scheme, page 42) and will include 58 Local Education Authorities, 1,000 secondary schools and a third of all secondary pupils by September 2001. The early evidence suggests that the schools in the most challenging circumstances in EiC are making the fastest progress. We expect the programme to make an increasing impact in the years ahead.
- **Excellence Clusters** are being established in seven areas: based on the experience of the EAZ programme and Excellence in Cities, they will promote high standards in pockets of disadvantage outside the major inner cities, such as the West Cumbrian coastal towns or Folkestone in Kent. We intend to expand this programme by announcing four more clusters to start in September 2001 and to include more areas over the next three years.

4.54 Each of these area-focused programmes will be crucial to achieving high standards across the country. However, we also need to target individual schools which face particular challenges, whether within those areas or outside them. We recently introduced a new programme, supported by £32 million, through which each of over 500 low attaining secondary schools in the country receive additional funding in return for a practical Raising Achievement Plan. Regular, constructive monitoring by OFSTED will help them to learn from best practice and adopt practical, effective approaches.

4.55 Some of the lowest attaining schools in the country are secondary modern schools in areas where a selective system still exists. We want to encourage more partnerships between grammar schools and secondary moderns in the future so that they can share expertise and learn from each other, as will happen in Ripon and Folkestone. We will provide additional funding to encourage this collaboration and in due course to extend it to all selective areas.

4.56 Of those schools which are found to be failing about 80 per cent are turned round successfully. The average time it takes for a school to emerge from special measures has fallen. Encouragingly, once schools have been turned round OFSTED's evidence indicates that they continue to improve. Four in five of those that are not turned round are closed, with neighbouring schools expanding to take the pupils. We see the expansion of successful schools as a key means of addressing failure and are prepared to support effective plans for doing so.

4.57 More recently we have made the City Academy option (described in paragraph 4.20) available to tackle historic underperformance. The proposal for external sponsors to take responsibility for a school against a fixed-term contract for 5–7 years (set out in paragraph 4.23) will provide a further option.

4.58 Only where a critical education presence in a community is necessary for purposes of regeneration and other options are unavailable should Fresh Start be considered. To date, it has been used for just 3 per cent of failing schools. This will never be straightforward but we cannot countenance a situation where a school is continuing to fail and no action is taken. If a Fresh Start does not succeed within a reasonably defined period (subject to consultation, we believe that this should be three years), it will be necessary to close the school and make whatever arrangements are necessary to transfer the pupils to the nearest available successful schools. Our simple but important principle is that the priority must be to ensure that pupils get a good education as soon as possible.

… And we will go further to support the schools facing the biggest problems

4.59 As these policies are put in place we expect to be able to see significant and sustained improvement in the vast majority of secondary schools in challenging circumstances. However, for a small number of schools in exceptionally challenging circumstances which, for example, are sited in extremely disadvantaged communities, have very high pupil mobility or a large number of asylum seekers, we intend to develop an option which is more radical still. Starting this year we intend as a pilot to offer substantial additional support and funding to about 8 or 10 well-managed secondary schools in these particularly difficult circumstances.

BARKING AND DAGENHAM VOCATIONAL PATHWAYS

This project has developed pre-vocational pathways in specific industrial areas of art and technology, such as print, engineering, industrial model-making or catering. The approach uses vocational GCSEs in eight secondary schools to emphasise the knowledge and skills of the field, while meeting the assessment criteria for the syllabus. The aim is to provide a thorough and high standard of technical education to exploit fully the potential of GCSE to enable the maximum number of pupils to gain success and recognition.

Pupils use industrial standards and equipment, while working to assignments which make commercial demands and provide access to the full range of grades A*–G. For example, one pupil studying Industrial Production GCSE as part of the Design and Technology College at the Warren Comprehensive School designed a highly innovative double action clamp, using precision tooling techniques and achieved an A* GCSE. The school is currently seeking a patent for his design.

Results from the project have been very encouraging, with schools reporting attainment results above predicted scores for project pupils. Additionally, schools report that pupils' attendance and standards of work have been driven up in other subjects.

4.60 The pilot will include a strong emphasis on much smaller classes and more flexible approaches to the use of time. We want teachers who choose to work in these extremely challenging circumstances to have additional support and pupils to benefit from an extended learning day and weekend and holiday learning.

WE WILL PROMOTE GREATER EQUALITY ...

4.61 These plans to improve all secondary schools will make significant inroads into the unacceptable inequality of opportunity which exists currently. There is no doubt that high expectations, focusing on individuals and examining comparative data are all essential.

4.62 Our plans to raise standards will also close the attainment gap for children from Caribbean, Pakistani, Bangladeshi and some other backgrounds, who have tended to be poorly served by their experience of school. There is often no lack of ability or aspiration in these children or their families; circumstances have conspired to limit their attainment. Through a combination of general and targeted policies, those circumstances can be changed. The recent Youth Cohort Study data (see Chapter 1) shows significant gains, on which we can build.

Targeted measures will include:
- A rigorous approach to monitoring the progress of ethnic minority pupils, and to setting targets for underperforming groups of pupils, aided by the increasing effectiveness of national and local level data analysis.
- A focus on the progress of black and other ethnic minority pupils in Excellence in Cities. With OFSTED, which is investigating the attainment of black pupils, we will develop a range of ways in which schools can engage them better, working with their families, with supplementary schools and with Beacon schools which are succeeding in allowing ethnic minority pupils to perform at the highest levels.
- A continued drive to tackle inequalities of attainment through the Ethnic Minority Achievement Grant, which is now worth over £150 million a year, and increasingly integrated within our wider drive to raise standards.
- Setting the highest standards of teaching for pupils for whom English is their second language, through linking it closely to the literacy strategy in primary and lower secondary education.
- Better induction of children who come as refugees or asylum seekers to England through intensive courses and support.

WE WILL SUPPORT INDIVIDUAL CHILDREN WHO MUST OVERCOME SOCIAL PROBLEMS...

4.63 We want to pilot a means of targeting funding to individual pupils whose own social circumstances are exceptionally challenging. Pupil Learning Credits will provide the secondary schools which these pupils attend, with extra funding, to enable the schools to offer them, both within the school day and outside it, the kind of opportunity that many more advantaged pupils take for granted: extra music tuition, museum and theatre visits, as well as extra support in the core curriculum if it is necessary. The pilot will involve a small number of schools in Excellence in Cities areas or Excellence Clusters with very high levels of pupils on free school meals. We will announce the details shortly.

4.64 The pilot will examine the quality of the provision, the benefits to the pupils and schools involved and, equally importantly, the use of the Pupil Learning Credits as a means of targeting funding precisely to the pupils in need of support. If it were to be successful, it would have important lessons, both for tackling disadvantage and for funding education. It is part of our work to ensure that funding follows the pupil and that education is tailored to the needs of the student.

WE ARE TACKLING DISAFFECTION ...

4.65 Over recent years pupil behaviour has improved significantly as OFSTED recognised in 1998–99. In some schools, especially those in challenging circumstances, it remains a significant problem. The Chief Inspector of Schools' 1999–2000 annual report indicates that last year there was the first small rise in behaviour problems for some time and that in some schools even good teachers are severely tested by some of the behaviour pupils bring with them into the school. We have recognised the importance of tackling this issue not just for the benefit of the poorly behaved pupils themselves who, left unchallenged, could become seriously disaffected but also for other pupils in their classes whose education is disrupted.

4.66 For the first time we have a fully-funded, comprehensive programme for tackling indiscipline, disaffection and disruption. It provides extra resources to schools which are willing to admit pupils who have caused trouble elsewhere, additional support staff in schools and provision for those who are excluded. We will be investing more than £200 million each year through the Standards Fund, the Children's Fund and Connexions over the next three years to tackle disruptive behaviour, exclusion and truancy and to support the most vulnerable children in our society. This compares to just £17 million in 1996–97.

4.67 In-school units, where pupils who are disrupting the classroom can be quickly removed from lessons and can get intensive support to improve their behaviour and to catch up, have proved their value. We are therefore funding schools to establish 1,000 Learning Support Units. Learning Mentors are also playing an important role in solving behaviour problems before they become so severe that exclusion is necessary. Where good alternatives like these have been in place for over a year, schools report significant improvements in behaviour and attainment.

4.68 While the number of pupils permanently excluded from school is falling from the excessive levels we saw in the mid-90s, there is now improved provision for those pupils who used, all too often, to become involved in crime, drugs or other anti-social behaviour when excluded.

4.69 But we know that there are youngsters whose behaviour is unacceptable and whose presence in the school causes major discipline and educational problems for others. We have therefore made clear that headteachers must be able permanently to exclude pupils whose behaviour is seriously disruptive to other pupils, in the interests of good discipline in the school and the learning of the majority of pupils. Where pupils are excluded, we have ensured that Education Authorities have the capacity to provide them with a full-time educational programme. There are now 1,000 more places and 250 more teachers working with excluded pupils in out-of-school units (Pupil Referral Units) than in 1997 and a full-time education will be provided for all excluded pupils by 2002. We are determined that wherever possible excluded pupils get back on track and make appreciable steps in learning. We will establish a national network of Pupil Referral Units to share best practice in educating excluded pupils. The old approach, which offered such young people only two or three hours tuition a week, left them no prospect of improving their behaviour and too much time to drift into trouble or a life of crime.

4.70 However, we also know that much misbehaviour arises from indiscipline and lack of interest in the home. We will therefore seek to strengthen the hand of heads and teachers in dealing with parents whose children's behaviour or attendance at school is unacceptable. The joint efforts of the Home Office and the DfEE, in conjunction with Education Authorities and schools, is beginning to pay dividends as police and education welfare staff join together in using the new powers available to them to deal with persistent truancy and misbehaviour.

... AND WE WILL PROVIDE INDIVIDUALISED SUPPORT FOR STUDENTS

4.71 We are also putting in place additional support for young people in the most challenging city areas. The new Excellence Challenge programme, an integral part of Excellence in Cities and in future of Education Action Zones and Excellence Clusters, will from September 2001 ensure that young people from areas of disadvantage with the potential to reach higher education get the support they need to achieve their full potential, starting when they are 14 and going through until they enter higher education. This is an important way of extending opportunity where it previously did not exist. There will be a strand of the Excellence Challenge dedicated to ensuring that more of the most able young people in those areas from maintained schools and colleges can enter the universities with the most demanding entry requirements. Opportunity Bursaries are being introduced as part of the Excellence Challenge, to support young people from these areas in higher education. Mentoring will also be an important part of this work. We want to expand substantially the National Mentoring Pilot Project, which provides training and a small stipend to undergraduates who choose to become mentors to 14–16 year olds at risk or in need of additional encouragement.

4.72 The Education Action Zones of East Middlesbrough and East Cleveland provide a good example of how the National Mentoring Pilot Project can work. Ninety-six students from the University of Teesside have already proved themselves to be very successful in their mentoring relationships with pupils. Children from 9 schools have been involved and there is growing evidence that the programme has a substantial impact upon pupils' exam grades.

4.73 Young people need effective support and guidance particularly as they reach the end of their school careers and take decisions about their future. The new Connexions Service, which is being progressively implemented across the country from 2001, focuses on the 13–19 age group to ensure a continuity of support is in place across this key transition point. Its central aim is to provide all teenagers with the help and support they need to prepare for the transition to work and adult life.

4.74 As well as web-based and telephone services, there will be a range of Connexions Service Personal Advisers including those working with young people who require more intensive help and support in dealing with personal, family and other problems getting in the way of their learning achievement. Many Connexions Service Personal Advisers will operate in schools and colleges building on and strengthening existing pastoral support arrangements. In Excellence in Cities schools Connexions Personal Advisers and Learning Mentors will work side by side, complementing each others' skills and knowledge base and linking in with external agencies.

4.75 This combination of reforms will transform the prospects of all young people, especially those from disadvantaged backgrounds. It will open entry to higher education and high-quality workplace training and ensure more than ever before that it is based on merit rather than background or place of birth.

WE WILL PROMOTE 'EDUCATION WITH CHARACTER'

4.76 Academic achievement is clearly crucial both to ensure that individuals have a range of options when they finish school and to ensure the future success of society as a whole. But no-one believes it is the only important outcome of schooling. It is also important that pupils learn to know right from wrong; to get along with their fellow pupils, whatever their background; to work in teams; to make a contribution to the school as a community; and to develop positive attitudes to life and work. This is important, not just for their capacity to take control of their own lives and to contribute to their family and community, but also to the success of the emerging new economy. Employers increasingly emphasise, not just academic qualifications, but skills and attitudes such as entrepreneurship, motivation, teamwork, creativity and flexibility.

4.77 This combination of skills, attitudes and habits of the mind we have called 'education with character'. Perhaps the most important means of ensuring pupils develop character in this sense is the ethos of the school they attend. All the evidence suggests that where schools develop a positive, respectful and can-do ethos not only do pupils develop better as rounded people, they are also likely to achieve higher academic standards. Hence the importance we attach to school ethos. To ensure it is given the attention it deserves we will:

- Discuss with OFSTED how inspection might give greater recognition to the importance of the ethos of a school in improving standards and discipline.
- Ask the National College for School Leadership and other providers of leadership training and development to give emphasis to training heads and prospective heads to understand how a positive ethos at school level can be established and sustained.

- Encourage schools to involve pupils much more actively in decisions, not just about their own individual learning, but about their class and their school as a whole. This can be done through the establishment of school councils, through regular surveys of pupil attitudes and a range of other means. The Barking and Dagenham Vocational Pathways scheme described earlier is an example.

4.78 All of these steps will be greatly reinforced by the introduction of Citizenship into the National Curriculum across the school system from September 2002 and by our continuing measures to ensure a broad and rich curriculum. Citizenship education will include political literacy, social and moral responsibility and community involvement. We recognise the important part that PE and sport play in encouraging a healthy lifestyle, increasing self-esteem, confidence and teamwork. And involvement in music and art can change the way children and young people feel, think and act, stimulate creativity and provide opportunities for self-expression, reflection and emotional development.

4.79 We have taken significant steps to increase the quality and spread of opportunities for secondary school children in these areas. The Music Standards Fund, Creative Partnerships, and the School Sports Co-ordinator programme, are all strengthening the framework for young people at school to enjoy rounded and varied learning experiences that will equip them more fully for the adult world. We are pleased to see that there has been an elevenfold increase in entries for the GCSE short course in Religious Education.

ASHLEY SPECIAL SCHOOL COUNCIL, HALTON

Ashley school has placed emphasis on developing citizenship at the heart of its activities. It has had a school council for nine years, which is central to the life of the school. A number of supporting committees ensure that most pupils have a chance to be directly involved. Students receive training for their roles in these committees. Staff supporting the council/committee meetings ensure that the learning opportunities of council/committee are integral to individuals' learning programmes.

The full school council meets weekly in a purpose fitted council chamber in the school. The school was the first special school to receive an Eco-Schools Award and pupils have been to both the Houses of Parliament and to Brussels to talk to MPs and MEPs. The school has been awarded the Schools Curriculum Award 2000.

The sculptor, David Gross, worked with pupils to make a large sculpture with symbols representing the rights and responsibilities of the school community as recorded in the School Charter–*A corporate commitment to justice and global citizenship*.

4.80 In sport in particular, the measures described earlier in paragraph 3.26 are making a major improvement to school sport provision. The Specialist Sports Colleges are Centres of Excellence spreading good practice throughout the education system, and we have introduced a target that there will be at least 150 of them by 2004. We are investing additional resources to create opportunities for young people to train in sport leadership and citizenship and to encourage them to volunteer; and £50 million supported by the New Opportunities Fund for outdoor activities with a focus on personal development for 16 year olds. We have also put in place protection for school playing fields, preventing their sale. Taken together, these steps amount to a powerful package of support for school sport.

4.81 Other steps we will take to build character include:
- Ensuring good work experience opportunities for all secondary pupils and a growing range of opportunities for work place learning from 14.
- Further extending the range of out-of-school learning opportunities available, especially in sports, arts, music and drama.
- Developing Creative Partnerships between schools and arts organisations in deprived areas to open up a wider variety of out-of-school learning opportunities.
- Developing further the range of mentoring schemes which are available.
- Encouraging across the 14–19 age group the opportunity for pupils to complete awards such as the Duke of Edinburgh Award which accredits the various aspects of character building. It offers pupils accreditation at bronze, silver and gold level for achievement in four areas: a new skill, a sport, community service and an expedition.

- Expanding the programme of summer activities for 16 year olds, particularly focused on outdoor adventure activities. We are investing £10 million in extended pilot projects before the programme is rolled out nationally from 2002, supported by the New Opportunities Fund and integrated closely with the Connexions Service.
- Offering all pupils from 5–16 an entitlement to 2 hours of PE and sport within and beyond the curriculum with increased opportunities to play competitive games.
- Through Culture Online, offering the opportunity for young people to develop their skills through interactive workshops, commissions, and events, working with established leaders in the creative fields, as well as develop their understanding of culture by working with the best cultural organisations in the country.
- Ensuring through individual pupil-level target-setting that these developments link well with the academic and vocational curriculum and ensure each pupil has a rounded education.

4.82 Taken together, the proposals in this chapter will combine to produce the longer term transformation of secondary education: higher standards; greater diversity of provision; greater equality of outcome; schools with the most serious problems improving; and every child able to achieve his or her potential across a wide range of activities.

CHAPTER 5
TEACHING – A 21st CENTURY PROFESSION

FOR TEACHERS

We will:

- continue our reforms of initial teacher training by creating new routes into teaching, so that training to teach can be part of undergraduate degrees;
- implement a recruitment and retention package for schools in the most challenging circumstances;
- introduce a package of support for teachers' professional development backed by a total of £92 million;
- continue to build new career paths for teachers, including by developing joint appointments of teachers to schools and higher education;
- support teachers to teach by cutting unnecessary burdens, bureaucracy and administration and investing in support staff and ICT; and
- continue to increase rewards for teachers to reflect their key role in society, with substantial new investment in performance pay between 2002 and 2004.

5.1 Schools and those who work in them are the real engine for improvement in education. That is why the teaching profession remains at the heart of all our proposals. In the Green Paper *Teachers: meeting the challenge of change* published in December 1998, we set out our vision for teaching:

"At the heart of what teachers do will remain the good, well-taught lesson – which has proved its effectiveness. But many new possibilities are emerging. Throughout the 20th century teachers had to choose between prioritising the needs of large groups or following up the diverse needs of individuals. Now for the first time they can do both.

New technology can add new dimensions to lessons, improving both effectiveness and presentation… Pupils' capacity to undertake independent research is being dramatically enhanced. Pupils' homes can be networked to schools. Teachers, through interactive technology, will be able to teach their traditional lessons to pupils not just in one location but several. New technologies are giving pupils with Special Educational Needs improved access to learning. None of this is wishful thinking: it is already beginning to happen.

In the end, however, it is the quality of teaching and the support available to teachers which will make the difference. The increasing numbers of teaching assistants and support professionals in schools will change approaches to teaching and learning…"

5.2 We want to make these new possibilities a reality for all teachers – so that they can make their full contribution, individually and collectively, to the progress of the education service as a whole. All teachers should have opportunities to update their skills, exploit modern technology to the full and develop new ways of working. The challenge is to make the best practice of some schools, the norm in every school.

5.3 This may seem an ambitious vision but it would be a mistake to overlook how far the teaching profession has already advanced towards its realisation. There is evidence throughout the system that teachers are making real changes.

- OFSTED reports more satisfactory or better lessons than ever before.
- Schools are focused on classroom practice and standards, and there is much better evidence about what works and much more sharing of ideas.
- Recent progress, especially at primary level, has raised expectations; and target-setting at school, class and pupil level has been enthusiastically adopted throughout the school system. Performance management is being put in place in all schools.
- Teachers are increasingly reaping benefits from working with a range of other staff including classroom assistants, learning support staff and Learning Mentors. And more schools are working with external partners such as other schools, businesses, community organisations and other public services, often innovating as a result.
- Teachers' experiences play a greater part in forming policy and practice – through national programmes such as Beacon schools and active consultative processes, such as the Learning from Success conferences.
- The establishment of the General Teaching Council and the National College for School Leadership means that powerful new institutions can express the voice of teachers and school leaders.

5.4 The changing economy is increasingly placing new demands on professionals in every field. In the 20th century, the professional could often expect to be treated as an authority, whose judgement was rarely questioned, and who was therefore rarely held to account. Despite this, professional judgements were not always based on evidence, and particularly in the public sector, services were arranged to suit the producer rather than the user.

5.5 Teaching, by contrast, is already in many ways a 21st century profession. More perhaps than any other, the teaching profession accepts accountability, is open to the contributions that others can make and is keen to seek out best practice. Teachers know that they are there to serve pupils and their parents and that they need:

- To have high expectations of themselves and of all pupils.
- To focus on classroom practice and take personal and collective responsibility for improving their skills and subject knowledge.
- To exercise informed professional judgement, basing their decisions as far as possible on data and evidence and fully exploiting modern technology.
- To accept accountability, above all, for the results of their students.
- To welcome the contribution that governors, parents, business and other partners can make to successful education.
- To promote innovation and increasingly to contribute, individually and collectively, to the development and progress of the service as a whole.

5.6 The vision of the 1998 Green Paper may not yet be realised but progress towards it is remarkable. The combination of rising standards and funding and growing acceptance of accountability means that the relationship between teachers and Government can be built more than ever before on trust. For example, now that the data systems, target-setting and the framework for school improvement are in place, we can greatly enhance the role that school self-evaluation plays in the inspection process. In this climate, in partnership with teachers, we will take forward the agenda of reform set out in the Green Paper and complete the modernisation of the teaching profession.

REFORMING INITIAL TEACHER TRAINING

5.7 We made it an early priority to ensure that new teachers are able to make an immediate impact in their first post. So we began a significant reform of initial teacher training: implementing a National Curriculum to establish high standards, and then crucially, aligning it fully with the National Literacy and Numeracy Strategies. We have employed Regional Directors from the two National Strategies to focus specifically on initial teacher training.

5.8 This has greatly improved primary teacher training, so that for the first time, we can have confidence that all trainee teachers are being taught best practice in teaching English and mathematics. At the same time, we have through the Teacher Training Agency ensured that more direct use is made of OFSTED inspection of initial teacher training establishments, to hold providers accountable for the quality of their training. The Teacher Training Agency has reduced and in extreme cases closed down low-quality provision. We have linked the funding of training to quality, so that the best at teacher training now train more teachers.

5.9 In support of this, we are introducing tests to ensure that trainee teachers have good occupational mathematics, English and ICT skills. And we continue to ensure that they spend the majority of their training working in schools, developing and practising their skills in the classroom, so that by the time they qualify they will be effective with their classes. After training, a new induction year with a reduced 90 per cent teaching commitment gives new teachers the chance to consolidate their training and prove themselves in the classroom, and provides a platform for them to carry on developing their skills throughout their careers.

5.10 Alongside this, we have expanded school-centred initial teacher training, where schools rather than higher education institutions take the lead. We have enlarged the Graduate Teacher Programme, which offers salaried school-based initial teacher training for mature students, from 84 places in 1997 to 1,680 in 2001, and increased incentives for schools and trainees. We have identified a first group of Training Schools to provide high-quality, professional and innovative forms of initial teacher training in a school setting.

5.11 Taken together, these reforms have greatly improved the quality of initial teacher training. OFSTED has found that the standard of teaching of those in their induction year is almost as high as that of the profession as a whole. Data from the TTA show that satisfaction levels amongst trainee teachers are now high, and more trainees are training in establishments which received the highest inspection grades (65 per cent in 1999 compared to 56 per cent in 1997).

5.12 We want to continue to embed these reforms. We believe that there are a number of options for undergraduate teacher training. First, for existing BA and BEd courses, which lead to qualified teacher status, we wish to consider whether we should offer a training salary and waive tuition fees for students when they reach their fourth year. Secondly, and on the basis of revised undergraduate courses, we wish to consider whether we should move to a salaried fourth year, along the lines of the Graduate Teacher Programme. A third option for undergraduate courses would be to allow the award of Qualified Teacher Status to exceptional fourth year students, who could then be paid as teachers before the completion of their degree. We also wish to explore whether we should offer all undergraduates opportunities to take up placements as Teaching Associates during their degree, depending on the timing of university and school terms.

5.13 We also wish to explore a new route to achieving Qualified Teacher Status, which would allow undergraduates on traditional academic degrees to take education modules as part of their degree so as to take part of a PGCE while still an undergraduate.We intend to pilot this final option in a number of universities. If an undergraduate could take, say, three education modules as part of an 18 module three-year degree and those modules could count towards both their degree and qualified teacher status, then they could make good progress towards a PGCE while doing their undergraduate degree. Where subject demands meant that students could not take any or many education modules in place of subject-related units, these could be provided in summer sessions.

5.14 A student who opted to do a PGCE in this way could be paid a training salary in installments while still an undergraduate. Training could then be completed in a reduced period of time in school, through arrangements similar to the Graduate Teacher Programme or other flexible routes, so that the new teacher earns a salary after three years rather than four.

5.15 Piloting this model will enable us to explore the practicalities further – for example, assuring the quality of teaching practice in schools; examining how much more training is needed after graduation before the award of qualified teacher status can be made; and the implications for other routes into teaching such as the four-year BEd. Subject to the success of the pilots, we intend to develop this new approach as a major route into teaching.

RECRUITING TEACHERS TO MAKE A DIFFERENCE

5.16 The Government has developed a programme to recruit and retain sufficient teachers of quality, in an increasingly competitive labour market. Teaching is by far the biggest recruiter of graduates in the country and faces fierce competition. Over the last generation, teacher supply has only been solved as a problem during economic recession. We are putting in place measures to solve it effectively in a period of sustained economic growth.

5.17 The work described here to improve the quality of teacher training will have an impact on teacher recruitment. We have introduced a new £6,000 training salary, which is paid to postgraduate trainee teachers while they train, and made training more flexible and adaptable to individuals' needs. £4,000 'golden hellos' in key shortage subjects also provide a strong incentive for recruitment, as does exemption from tuition fees.

5.18 In addition, we are piloting new paths into teaching. We are providing ongoing professional training for teaching assistants and expanding their routes into the profession. Our new Fast Track scheme, where trainee teachers with high potential and talented qualified teachers can make faster career progress, is another scheme that will attract able graduates. It has already generated great interest. We are encouraging currently under-represented groups to move into teaching through all these routes.

5.19 We believe that offering undergraduates opportunities to work in schools while studying for their degree will help to attract them into teaching. We have introduced a programme of associate teachers – undergraduate and postgraduate students who spend time working in schools. Currently 900 students are part of our National Mentoring Pilot and we hope that significant numbers will consider becoming teachers.

5.20 The result of this is that we have reversed a declining trend of interest in teaching at a time of economic success and through campaigns led by the TTA, we are translating growing interest into solid applications. By the beginning of February 2001, over 115,000 people had made enquiries and over 50,000 had registered their details with the Teacher Training Agency, expressing interest in training to be a teacher and nearly 20,000 had applied for postgraduate teacher training (the equivalent figures for the previous year were 43,000, 19,000 and 17,900 respectively). The number of students in training is now rising significantly for the first time since 1992/93: there are now 2,250 more people training to be teachers than in January 2000. And there are almost 7,000 more teachers in service than in 1998.

5.21 We want to make teaching still more attractive, by giving extra support to those who commit to it as a career. For shortage subjects and areas of difficulty in recruitment, we will explore a scheme to assist new teachers who enter and remain in employment in the state education sector to pay off, over a set period of time, their student loans.

5.22 We also want to solve the problems in the places where it is hardest to recruit and retain staff. We want to make it a much more attractive option for teachers and headteachers to work in schools in challenging circumstances and we have taken action to help schools facing some of the greatest challenges. We now want to put in place specific measures to support them in recruiting and retaining staff. There are already many dedicated teachers deriving great professional satisfaction from their work in these schools, but it is not enough to rely on this. For the pupils at such schools, good headteachers and teachers are simply essential. Our full range of measures will provide:

- A dedicated recruitment and retention service offering professional advice.
- Much greater support for headteachers and senior managers provided by the National College for School Leadership. They will have access to mentoring by business people and excellent professional development and networking opportunities.
- Additional funding both through targeted programmes such as Excellence in Cities and Education Action Zones and direct to schools, to enable them to offer extra support to teachers.
- Tailored recruitment packages to suit different teachers at different stages of their careers, including pension enhancements and salary bonuses.
- Specialist training packages to help teachers meet the professional demands of teaching in challenging circumstances.

5.23 We also want to make it more attractive for teachers to work in some of our highest cost areas. There are now more on-the-job training places in Excellence in Cities schools in London. These places attract a training salary of £150 per week. We are making it possible for Local Education Authorities in high-cost housing areas to help teachers buy their first homes through obtaining funds from the Starter Home Initiative. We are now extending to other parts of the country facing shortages our successful London scheme using refresher courses to help people to return to teaching, backed by £2.5 million a year for the next two years.

5.24 We have also now introduced new flexibilities in pay. Schools will have complete discretion for the first time to offer recruitment and retention payments of up to £5,000 a year per teacher to help to tackle recruitment difficulties, particularly in high cost areas. New retention bonus packages, worth up to £15,000 per teacher, will help retain teachers in particularly challenging jobs by carrying forward allowances for periods of up to three years and paying them as a bonus at the end of the period.

5.25 Taken together with across the board increases in pay, new opportunities for good teachers to receive promotion to a new higher pay scale and increases in London allowances, we believe that this package of measures will significantly enhance schools' ability to recruit and retain teachers.

TALKING HEADS

Talking Heads is the interactive online community of the National College for School Leadership, and all headteachers in England are being invited to join. It allows headteachers to network with other school leaders and experts from this country and internationally and to debate freely and in confidence current professional issues. Comments from headteachers participating in the pilot of Talking Heads include:

- "Talking Heads is like meeting all your other headteacher colleagues... and being able to debate when you choose, for as long as you choose, the issues that are important to you."
- "The biggest benefit is that it ends the isolation of being a Head... my confidence has increased and I feel that I'm part of a national network, rather than acting in isolation..."
- "The difference it's made to me... is having a whole load of Heads to speak to at the touch of a button, across the country... and to have someone to talk to, share my problems with and get immediate answers as well. There's always someone who's got some sort of solution out there."

ENHANCING PROFESSIONAL DEVELOPMENT

5.26 The working environment is changing at an unprecedented rate. Like every other profession, teaching must keep pace if we are to prepare children for a rapidly changing labour market. For teachers, as much as for their pupils, the issue is one of lifelong learning: the need to continuously build and update skills.

5.27 The power of high-quality professional development has been amply borne out by the Literacy and Numeracy Strategies. Last year alone, for example, all 18,000 primary headteachers received a day's training on literacy, 38,000 teachers received additional phonics training, 25,000 teachers were trained in how to teach writing and 6,000 primary schools received intensive support in the teaching of numeracy. Ninety-nine per cent of those who participated in numeracy training rated it as satisfactory or better. The system has never achieved anything like this volume and quality of professional development before.

5.28 Our consultation on teachers' professional development in 2000 made very clear that teachers want to keep their skills up to date and we will continue to invest in national strategic training priorities. The Key Stage 3 strategy is being piloted and will be available to all secondary schools from the next academic year. Over 200,000 teachers are registered for training in the use of ICT in the classroom, and some 74,000 have completed it.

5.29 Last year we launched opportunities for teachers in three new areas: to carry out research into best practice in teaching and learning; to visit other countries to see how they were tackling particular problems; and a new scheme gave teachers bursaries to spend on any professional development activities meeting their needs.

5.30 We want to extend these into future years as part of a new national strategy for professional development. This will be backed by £90 million over three years for a series of development initiatives. One is a new opportunity for experienced teachers in challenging areas to take sabbaticals, allowing them to pursue development activities of value to them and their school. Another is increased professional development for teachers in their second and third years of teaching, building on the induction year.

5.31 Alongside these new programmes, we will spread across the school system the excellent practice in a number of schools of placing professional development at the heart of their approach to school improvement. Successful schools are always outward facing and committed to sharing best practice and seeking innovative thinking wherever they can find it. This vital process of networking and sharing knowledge is at the heart of teachers' professionalism because it involves both learning from what works and contributing to the pool of professional knowledge. We will continue to emphasise the value that can come from teachers learning from each other – through observing lessons, feedback, coaching and mentoring – which many teachers find the most effective way to improve their practice.

IMPROVING LEADERSHIP

5.32 Good leadership is an essential component of a successful school. We know that good leadership from governing bodies, headteachers and their senior team creates an environment in which teachers can give of their best. We are committed to giving school leaders the best possible preparation and development.

So:
- We have launched the National College for School Leadership. We want to establish it as a world class institution providing inspiration and support to all school leaders and potential leaders. It will offer the very best development opportunities, online and face to face (see *Talking Heads* opposite).
- The National College will link to the growing worldwide network of similar institutions so that leaders here learn from and share with the best practitioners globally and will be a voice for school leaders in the debate about how to bring about further improvement over the years ahead.
- We are reviewing the national development framework for leadership. The revised National Professional Qualification for Headship has already attracted a record 3,000 applicants since its launch last year. We are improving training for new heads, and refining the popular and successful Leadership Programme for Serving Heads.

THE IMPACT OF AN ADVANCED SKILLS TEACHER (AST)

Jackie Beere is an AST at a secondary school where she has introduced a new 'Learning to Learn' course as part of a national research project. She is now leading a team of teachers helping Year 7 students to take control of their own learning. In a number of ways, the work is having an impact on the whole school as a result of training delivered by Jackie in October. She is delivering similar training in other schools to all phases with a very positive response from teachers.

5.33 School leaders have played a vital role in bringing about the changes of the last few years. We have recognised the importance of school leadership in a number of ways, including by setting up the new wider leadership group pay scale. We have also recognised the importance of leaders of teaching and learning, such as Advanced Skills Teachers. We have given more scope for schools to use pay to recognise the importance of headteachers. The top of the pay scale has been increased sharply: in 1997 headteachers could be paid up to £57,400; from April a top headteachers could receive up to £78,800, and in exceptional circumstances much more than this.

BUILDING NEW CAREER PATHS

5.34 One of the important effects of our reforms has been to create new career paths for teachers. Gone are the days when the only way for a teacher to make progress in his or her career was to move out of the classroom and into management. We need top class leaders and managers in our schools more than ever. But our pay reforms provide a route for all teachers to be promoted to a new pay scale by performing well in the classroom, without having to reduce their teaching commitments as a result.

5.35 We have also introduced important new roles for teachers. One is the new grade of Advanced Skills Teacher (AST) for some of the very best classroom practitioners, who can earn up to £44,600 (£47,600 in London) in return for taking on additional responsibilities for spreading best practice. They also have a major role to play in interchange with and informing practice in higher education institutions. OFSTED evaluation shows how these excellent teachers are beginning to be seen as important figures in school improvement and we intend to increase the number of ASTs sharply.

5.36 School improvement measures have given teachers other new career opportunities to spread expertise across schools, for example as literacy and numeracy consultants or leading mathematics or literacy expert teachers helping to model best practice for colleagues. Over 40 per cent of primary teachers have now been to a demonstration of a daily mathematics lesson taught by a skilled colleague and had the opportunity to discuss its implications for their practice.

5.37 All of these developments are making teaching a more vibrant and varied career than it has been for many years. We want to continue to open up new paths for teachers, so that all teachers are able to progress in their careers while making a variety of different contributions to the education system. Many teachers are passionate about their subject and would like to be able to research and write about it as well as teach it. Meanwhile in universities there is strong demand for people who, in addition to expertise in their subject, are excellent teachers. We would therefore like to see the development of joint appointments, which would involve a teacher being on the staff of both a university and a school. We intend to explore the practicalities of piloting this with a number of leading universities and schools.

5.38 Similarly, we intend to pilot a university fellowship scheme that will let school teachers with real expertise in their subject take a secondment to a university. This would enable them to spend a term or so researching their subject and perhaps embarking on a higher degree. Both these schemes, apart from their intrinsic merit, would have the benefit of strengthening the links between the university and school sectors to the advantage of both.

ENABLING TEACHERS TO TEACH

5.39 We want teachers to be able to focus exclusively on their central professional tasks of teaching, preparation and assessing pupils' work and on their own professional development. And they must be able to achieve a balance between their very strong commitment to their profession and their pupils, and their own personal life. If this is to be achieved, we must:

- Keep the administrative burden on teachers to a minimum.
- Increase the numbers of staff supporting teachers inside and outside the classroom.
- Capitalise on the potential of new technology to ease the pressures on teachers.

5.40 Mentors, as in the Excellence in Cities programme, are also helping to ensure that teachers can concentrate on their key tasks, rather than being diverted by problems outside school. Pastoral care remains a key area within schools, but teachers can be helped if their students have mentors with the time and expertise to address problems which affect educational processes, but are outside the classroom teacher's remit.

5.41 There is significant variation in the extent to which teachers feel supported at school level and the effectiveness with which schools manage teachers' time. We intend to research this further to see what lessons can be learned and shared but already action is in hand on a wide range of fronts to support teachers.

Streamlining administration

5.42 We know that there is nothing more frustrating for schools than to have to deal with paperwork and bureaucracy. We have listened to their views and taken action. We are cutting by a third the number of documents and by a half the number of pages we send automatically to schools during the current school year, with a panel of headteachers and teachers advising on what should be sent. Last term, primary schools were sent 490 pages of material – a reduction of 1,170 pages compared to the same term in the previous year; and secondary schools were sent 254 pages – a reduction of 737 pages. These measures will save a typical school over 200 hours of paperwork each year – equivalent to over a month's work for one person.

5.43 We are radically simplifying the Standards Fund for 2001–02, to streamline the way that the money gets to schools. There will be no more bidding, simpler monitoring, much less form-filling and greater flexibility – along with considerably more funding. This should save more than three weeks' work in a typical school. We are developing good practice guidelines for headteachers on how management and administration can be streamlined within schools. We are also sharply reducing the amount of data we collect from schools.

5.44 We have also introduced 'light touch' OFSTED inspections for successful schools, which will reduce the workload connected with inspection. The range of measures described below that we have introduced to provide additional support staff in schools and for the use of ICT will also make a significant impact in reducing teachers' workload.

5.45 In addition, we are helping small schools with an additional £80 million a year for administrative support. The funds have been widely welcomed and are making a significant impact (see paragraph 3.9). We are encouraging schools to develop innovative approaches to sharing resources, such as pooling funding to make joint appointments. For example, some small schools have been able to take on shared ICT technicians, enabling them to develop both curriculum and management information systems, so improving effectiveness as well as reducing bureaucracy. Others have taken on shared specialist subject teachers, with the added benefit of providing some time for other teachers to carry out planning and assessment away from the classroom. And schools will be able to join together to use the funds to take on shared bursars to relieve the burden of administrative work from teaching staff.

5.46 We know that there is more to be done.

So we will:

- Discuss with OFSTED how to achieve further substantial reductions in the bureaucracy associated with inspection within a few months.
- Transform how information is managed and shared across the whole school system. The introduction of a common data set and common standards for electronic systems will ensure data have to be input only once and can be transferred at a touch of a button. The same data will be shared by national departments, agencies and Local Authorities, cutting out form-filling and duplicate requests.
- Work with Local Education Authorities to ensure they adopt rigorous new standards for controlling what they send to schools and the demands they make.
- Strip out any obsolete or unnecessarily burdensome legislative requirements.

5.47 We believe that taken together, these measures will have a substantial impact on reducing the amount of unnecessary work that teachers undertake. But we are determined to continue supporting teachers in other ways too.

Increasing support staff

5.48 Using support staff in schools, whether in the classroom in the case of teaching assistants, for example, or outside it, in the case of bursars and other administrative staff, can make a profound difference for teachers. By giving schools greater security in their budgets over three years and guaranteeing the value of the School Standards Grant over the same period, we have given schools greater confidence to invest in extra teaching staff, or in support staff.

ONLINE MATERIAL FOR TEACHING AND LEARNING

The Government has commissioned whole courses in mathematics, Latin and Japanese for 11 year old pupils. This pilot will equip teachers and learners with modern resources and make courses available in schools where opportunities to learn some of these subjects did not previously exist. During the pilot, participants will be able to access a whole year's material in the three subjects. The courses will be evaluated throughout the year and plans for building on the pilot developed as a consequence.

5.49 In addition, we are funding the recruitment of extra teaching assistants and providing, for the first time, structured induction training for them so that they can support teachers more effectively in the classroom. The number of support staff in schools has increased by 24,000 since January 1997.

5.50 As well as administrative support for schools, and additional teaching support in the classroom, we are bringing Learning Mentors into schools to help children to deal with problems outside school that are affecting their learning. We will expand support of this type, and look to increase inter-agency working between schools and, for example, health and social services so that teachers are more able to focus on their core tasks, and pupils receive better services delivered seamlessly.

5.51 We will continue to invest so that schools can employ additional support staff. Over time we want to see continued significant increases in their numbers at both primary and secondary levels, so that overall pupil:adult ratios continue to improve. We believe that well-trained assistants working effectively alongside a teacher can help teachers to deliver effective lessons and so contribute significantly to pupil outcomes. Over time, we would also like to see time outside the classroom for planning and assessment become the norm for primary teachers.

Employing new technology

5.52 ICT has the potential to reduce teachers' workloads and to improve their effectiveness. We are investing in ICT to reduce burdens, providing web-based tools and services that can all now be accessed in one place through TeacherNet, and making teaching resources available through the National Grid for Learning. The Standards Site provides best practice resources for teachers (including for example worksheets and multimedia presentations), and TeacherNet will offer lesson plans and lesson planning tools so that teachers can draw on others' experiences. Teachers will be able to share new and imaginative ideas online, and as we develop digital content for the whole curriculum, the scope for teachers to draw down the most imaginative and creative programmes across the curriculum will be transformed. The pilot projects described in *Online Material for Teaching and Learning* are an early example of progress in this area.

5.53 But this by no means exhausts the potential of ICT as a tool for helping teachers. We will use it to provide more support for planning and preparing lessons. We will make available on the National Grid for Learning lesson planning tools that will help teachers in their preparation; and complete lesson plans prepared and used in the classroom by teachers which other teachers will be able to adapt and use for their own purposes.

5.54 Taken together, we believe that reduced bureaucratic burdens on teachers, together with new supporting combinations of assistants and technology, create exciting opportunities for innovative approaches to teaching which will increase the professional status of teachers. Growing numbers of classroom assistants have enabled two or more adults to work together in a single classroom under the direction of a teacher. Increasingly, new technology will allow schools to join together to conduct masterclasses, extend curriculum options and pool their resources to give pupils a richer learning experience.

5.55 Innovative schools have already reorganised their timetable so that groups of teachers with a shared professional interest can plan and prepare together; blocked whole days on the timetable for one-to-one teacher pupil consultations; and enhanced staffing levels to free greater time for professional development without disruption to pupils. We will promote, through the Standards Site and other means, this and other 'smart' approaches to the use of time.

REWARDING A KEY ROLE IN SOCIETY

5.56 We promised to reward good teachers and to offer good teachers better pay progression. The new pay structure has now been put in place, with higher salaries and better prospects. It is supported by the best part of a billion pounds this year and next to modernise the teaching profession, over and above the annual pay increases each year.

- Newly qualified teachers will earn £17,000 (£20,000 in Inner London) in 2001, compared to £14,500 in 1997. Senior managers will be eligible to earn up to £36,800, compared to £30,200 in 1997.
- The new upper pay scale will give good teachers an immediate pay increase of £2,000. Over 200,000 teachers have applied for threshold assessment to go onto the new scale and we expect most to be successful. They are eligible to go on to earn up to £31,000 (£34,000 in London), compared to a maximum of £24,000 for classroom teachers without management responsibility in April 2000. The best teachers in the classroom will be able to earn almost £45,000 as Advanced Skills Teachers.
- Alongside individual pay awards, we are also introducing a £60 million School Achievement Awards scheme to give pay bonuses for staff at good schools. The first Awards will be given this spring. Some 7,000 schools will be recognised for sustained improvement or achievement and the bonuses will be available to teaching and to non-teaching staff.

5.57 We believe that teaching is a key profession for our society in the 21st century. And our reforms mean that for the first time, teachers can also get the financial rewards for focusing on classroom teaching that this vital role deserves.

CHAPTER 6
THE CAPACITY TO DELIVER

6.1 The previous five chapters have set out a radical and long-term agenda for the future of our education system. Both the resources and, equally importantly, the capacity at every level in the system, need to be in place if that ambitious agenda is to be delivered.

6.2 In this chapter we deal first with the question of resources and second with building capacity.

RESOURCES

6.3 The Government's approach to public sector reform has consistently emphasised that money and modernisation go hand in hand. We are committed to ensuring that the investment will be there to enable necessary reform. All the evidence shows that a great deal of progress has been made.

6.4 The success is, at least in part, a result of the very significant extra investment made in schools. In real terms from April 2001 schools will receive on average £450 per pupil per year more than they did in 1997. Investment in school buildings has tripled over the same timescale from £683 million to £2.1 billion per year.

6.5 Furthermore, more resources are devolved to schools than ever before. Indeed, the degree of delegation to school level is greater in this country than in any other country in the world: we have increased it from around 79 per cent to 84 per cent of schools funding. This is not just a question of the delegation of the annual revenue budget. By 2003–04, we will be devolving £500 million a year of capital funding to schools, enabling governors and headteachers to improve the physical environment alongside teaching and learning. In fact, considerably more capital funding will have been devolved directly to schools over this period for them to use as they choose than the total of capital investment in the system in 1996–97.

6.6 We recognise that it took some time for the impact of our investment to be noticeable. As we put in place key reforms and the foundation for present successes and future achievement, the extra resources may not have been immediately apparent to those for whom they were intended. But we believe that the additional day-to-day funding for salaries, for extra teachers, for ICT hardware and software, for smaller class sizes, books and equipment are now visible and making a real impact on the ground.

6.7 As a result of the spending review announcement in July 2000 we will make further increases in funding, averaging in excess of 6 per cent each year over and above inflation between 1999–2000 and 2003–04. The spending plans for 2001–04 include:
- Over £10.2 billion more by 2003–04 on education and training in England than in 2000–01.
- Increased spending per pupil, bringing the total increase to around £700 per pupil over and above inflation between 1997–98 and 2003–04.
- A £7.8 billion capital programme over the three years.
- £540 million in 2001–02 rising to £570 million by 2003–04 in direct grants to schools for boosting standards in classrooms.

6.8 Moreover, the Prime Minister has made clear his commitment to the longest period of sustained growth in education expenditure for more than a generation. Spending on education as a proportion of national income will again be increased over the next Parliament. This ongoing investment will make possible successful reform and sustained improvement in pupil performance in a way that the historic pattern of short spurts of growth followed by retrenchment never could.

Distribution

6.9 In addition to making more resources available year on year, the Government is determined to reform the way in which funding for schools is distributed in order to improve its fairness and transparency.

6.10 In doing so, we want to ensure:
- A fair allocation of funding between authorities and between schools in authorities to reflect pupil needs.
- That the funds allocated by central Government for education are used for that purpose.
- That funding is properly matched to the separate responsibilities of Local Authorities and schools.

6.11 As the recent Green Paper, *Modernising Local Government Finance* published by the Department of the Environment, Transport and the Regions makes clear, current funding arrangements fall short of these aspirations.

6.12 Firstly, the distribution of funding between Education Authorities, through the Standard Spending Assessment arrangements, is widely regarded as unfair. Secondly, there is currently no way for central Government to guarantee that funding it intends for schools actually reaches them. Finally, the current system does not clearly separate out funding intended to go directly to schools, and funding intended for use by Local Education Authorities in support of the work of schools (such as co-ordination of services for pupils with Special Educational Needs or the provision of home-to-school transport).

6.13 The Government is consulting on proposals that school funding could be based on a simpler and more transparent formula. This could comprise a basic entitlement per primary or secondary school pupil, with enhancements for schools and pupils in Authorities where significant deprivation adds to the challenge of achieving high standards. It would also recognise that there are some areas where, for cost-of-living reasons, schools need to pay more to recruit and retain staff. Allocation of funds between schools would remain at local level with the Authority and its schools working together, since they best know what variations in funding are needed.

6.14 Crucially the proposals also involve much greater transparency to ensure that central Government money intended for education is used for education. Funding for schools and funding for Local Authorities would be separately identified. Authorities would be required to give both their council taxpayers and schools a full account of how that funding had been allocated to schools and what had been spent on Authorities' own services. They would be required to indicate the proportions provided by national Government and by locally-raised finance; and provide a comparison with the previous year. The greater transparency of these arrangements will improve the accountability of both Local Education Authorities and schools for the value for money they provide.

Improving school buildings

6.15 All schools have already benefited from increased capital investment, including the £1.3 billion capital which is being devolved directly to them from 2000–01 to 2003–04. In total, we have invested £5.4 billion since 1997. We are taking care to deploy all our capital resources to maximise their impact. We have for the first time set out a three-year programme of capital expenditure. After decades of neglect, we are using the resources and support systems of local government wisely and effectively to support this work. We have introduced Asset Management Plans so that every Local Education Authority demonstrates that resources are deployed strategically to make the biggest impact on the ground – and we are holding Authorities to account. In addition, we have developed public private partnerships to make better use than ever before of private sector skills and funding.

6.16 Almost 17,000 building projects have so far been supported in schools through the New Deal for Schools capital grant. Given the appalling state of many school buildings in 1997, a great deal of this extra capital has been spent on essential repairs. We are working urgently to bring the condition of all school buildings up to a standard fit for the 21st century – not least by eliminating reliance on outside toilets. But as we address the repairs backlog, we need also to move away from the patch and mend thinking of the past, brought about by eighteen years of neglect and under-investment. We need to modernise our schools so that they provide the very best learning environments for the community they serve. Over the next three years, capital investment of £7.8 billion will mean that more and more schools will have an environment suitable for learning in the 21st century. Already we are investing three times the level of capital in our schools compared with 1997, and current spending will increase by a further 50 per cent by 2003–04.

6.17 Schools in the future must support the changing nature of education and the increased role of schools at the heart of communities. The types of learning space needed in the future will be very different to most of those in place today. Schools must be a focus for learning for the whole community, fully accessible to all and providing modern and attractive facilities for learning for families and people of all ages. We are testing innovative ideas to develop new types of classroom to improve the learning experience and to harness the full potential of ICT. We want increasingly to think ahead and to design and create school buildings suitable for the transformed education service of the future. In short, we want to develop both the concept and the reality of the school of the future.

6.18 Research shows clear links between capital investment in schools and educational standards. Capital investment is one of the most powerful levers on teacher motivation, which in turn impacts on attainment levels. Investment in modern facilities also has a strong and positive influence on pupil motivation. We are making money available through an expanded New Deal for Schools programme for modernising schools, as well as for addressing urgent condition needs and giving schools some capital funds of their own. Over the next three years, 650 schools will be either replaced or substantially remodelled as a result of this investment, in addition to the 7,000 schools where other large building works will take place.

6.19 Many schools are also benefiting from the Private Finance Initiative. Twenty-one deals have been signed so far, and funding for a further 33 has been agreed in principle, bringing benefits to around 640 schools. The scale of activity here is increasing. Private finance deals can provide schools with modern learning environments, fully maintained over twenty-five to thirty years. They enable teachers to focus on teaching, using well-equipped classrooms and without the many distractions from maintaining poor buildings. We want to consider whether there is potential for allowing schools to use their devolved capital resources to finance future public private partnerships.

6.20 We are also cutting out bureaucracy and making it much easier for schools to access capital investment where it is most needed to raise standards. All Local Authorities are developing Asset Management Plans, in consultation with schools and dioceses, to identify and agree local priorities for capital investment. This is improving local decision-making and will enable schools to plan ahead with much greater certainty. We are also reforming the way that capital funding is provided for school places so that popular and overcrowded schools in growth areas can receive extra investment to provide additional learning space. Through discussion with the churches, we plan to streamline the way that voluntary aided schools receive funding for work on their premises. As part of this, we intend to reduce the contribution made by governing bodies to the costs of building work at these schools from 15 per cent to 10 per cent for capital items, and to remove the contribution altogether for revenue items. This will make life much easier for these schools and will further promote diversity.

6.21 City Learning Centres (see page 82) provide an example of what can be achieved when buildings are tailor-made to serve other schools and the wider community.

ICT

6.22 Information and Communications Technology has already brought transformation to many sectors of the economy. Increasingly it is changing the way schools work as well. Many schools – including a number highlighted in this document – are using ICT to change teaching and learning; to improve communication between teachers and parents; to assess and record pupil progress and set targets; to show best practice; to design, adapt and prepare teaching materials; to link with schools across the globe; and to put information at the fingertips of all their pupils. There is potential for ICT to offer pupils access to a wealth of digital content, including cultural and artistic material, and we are looking at a variety of ways of making this access easier, including through a 'virtual librarian'. These changes are in addition to those that enable streamlined management and administrative systems to free teachers to teach and headteachers to focus their energy on raising standards.

CITY LEARNING CENTRES

CLCs provide an example of the type of high-quality 21st century learning environments that are currently being created. A number of principles are guiding their development:

- Buildings are of high-quality and reflect their purpose through imaginative and innovative use of design solutions to make the building look modern and lively. Entrances and receptions should be visible and big enough to provide communal space.
- Building materials are from recycled sources or recyclable from sustainable sources. They meet the highest environmental standards, with excellent insulation. Energy use and health issues are considered throughout construction and manufacturing.
- The design is flexible, taking into account the need for rapid reorganisation, both day to day and in the longer term. The design caters for individuals of different sizes (infants to adults), as well as groups. Space takes account of the numbers of workstations and general work areas, allowing for minimal distractions.

Liverpool provides an example of how CLCs are helping schools and communities. It has four Centres - two started last year, with a further two Centres to start in September 2001.

The first two Centres are based n Shorefields Community School and St John Bosco High School. Both are in areas of disadvantage and each centre (or hub) will link to partner secondary schools which will operate as spokes - the Shorefields City Learning Centre will link to six spokes schools and the Bosco City Learning Centre to five. In both cases the bulk of the capital will be spent on the hub. Primary schools will also have access to the Centres. There will also be links with schools in Merseyside. In addition, the Centres will establish networks with the NGfL, HE and FE establishments and Community Grids for Learning.

Each Centre will open for 12–14 hours a day all year round. Management of the Centres will be the responsibility of a Management Board which will include representatives from the host school, partners and Local Education Authority.

The Centres will provide a full range of ICT facilities. At both sites, there is a cyber café, literacy and numeracy facilities, whole class access ICT areas and individual learning suites. The plan also proposes offering 'immersion' courses for pupils. At Bosco CLC, additional facilities include a performance space and music ICT area, Shorefields also includes a dedicated Design Technology area with CNC equipment.

6.23 There is a growing body of evidence which shows that the application of ICT in schools not only motivates pupils but also improves their performance. Recent research published by BECTa shows this powerfully at both primary and secondary levels. ICT, until recently an optional extra, often consigned to a particular IT lesson, is moving firmly into the mainstream and becoming a key lever in the drive to raise standards, motivate pupils and make teachers' workload more manageable.

6.24 The investment in ICT has been substantial. Between 1998 and 2004 we are investing some £1.8 billion in the National Grid for Learning and in ICT teacher training. The number of computers in schools has grown dramatically. As a result there is now one computer for every 13 pupils in primary schools and one for every 8 pupils at secondary level, and we are committed to further improvements. The increased investment has also increased connectivity with virtually every secondary and 86 per cent of primary schools now connected to the Internet (compared to only 17 per cent of primaries in 1998).

6.25 To ensure this investment is well used at school level, two further strands of activity are essential. The first is the development of software of real quality which is directly relevant to teaching and school administration. Government itself has a direct part to play and through such developments as the Standards Site, the National Grid for Learning, the Virtual College for School Leadership and the Virtual Teachers' Centre, materials and best practice are being widely disseminated. And the DfEE parents' website remains a popular and valuable guide through the system. Still more important is the work the Government is doing to encourage commercial organisations to provide software related to the National Curriculum and the challenges faced by schools. There has been real progress in recent years and a step-change in the quality and quantity of materials available can be expected in the next three or four years. All of this will play a key role in delivering the developing curriculum and the new models of teaching outlined in Chapters 4 and 5.

6.26 The second is investment in training teachers and headteachers to be able to use ICT effectively in their day-to-day work. Only if teachers can use the available technology effectively will it support our agenda for school improvement. Funding through the New Opportunities Fund has already enabled a very significant proportion of teachers to be trained in the use of ICT, and the Computers for Teachers scheme has supported teachers to buy their own computers.

6.27 These developments have laid the foundation for the next major leap. Further investment in hardware, connectivity, software and training will bring dramatic change. Once schools have broadband connections, the speed and quality of Internet working will be greatly enhanced. Our £10 million Classroom of The Future pilot scheme will enable schools in 12 areas to explore radically new and inspiring ways of delivering education.

6.28 Within the next five years we expect to see the use of ICT becoming routine in virtually every classroom; schools able to run their administrative systems electronically and integrate them with curriculum networks; and all communication between schools and Government becoming electronic. We also expect to see schools at the cutting edge advancing far beyond where we are currently and showing how ICT, used in combination with teachers and other skilled adults, can change the nature of the classroom experience and the organisation of the school day. Our proposed new category of advanced specialist school will lead the way but many of the changes will result from innovative heads and teachers applying ICT imaginatively to help solve the problems they face.

6.29 We are likely, for example, to see much more flexible use of time during the school day with a mix of traditional teaching methods, augmented by the presentational quality ICT allows, and more individualised and small group work; homework being set, done and marked online; teachers in one school teaching in teams with teachers from other schools; widespread sharing between schools of lesson plans linked to Schemes of Work; increased use of ICT-based assessment techniques and a vast growth in international collaboration offering, for example, every pupil learning French the opportunity for regular conversation with a native speaker. ICT will also enable every school to test the views of parents and pupils on proposed changes and to update the report to parents on their child's progress regularly while taking less, not more, teacher time.

6.30 The investment in ICT will therefore not merely raise quality and open up new possibilities, it will also reduce the time teachers spend on lower priority activities and free them to focus on improving pupil performance.

BUILDING CAPACITY

6.31 The successful implementation of radical reform has never been a matter merely of investment, important though that is. It is also crucially a matter of ensuring that at every level in the system there are people with skills, knowledge, understanding, time and attitudes which enable successful change to occur. In short, it is a matter of building capacity.

6.32 At the heart of the framework for continuous improvement which we have put in place is the self-governing school responsible for the performance of its pupils, in control of its staffing and budget and planning its own future development. The keys to capacity at school level are the capability of governors, teachers and other staff, excellent continuing professional development and the quality of leadership and management. That is why we have emphasised these issues in the previous chapter.

6.33 Governors of course provide a vital source of support for heads and teaching staff, but it is also crucial that staff know where outside the school to turn for advice, assistance, best practice and inspiration. Local Authorities have a key part to play in these respects (see paragraph 6.52 onwards) but schools need a variety of sources to turn to. For these reasons we have put in place and will continue to develop many forms of collaborative networks among schools: Education Action Zones, Excellence in Cities partnerships, Beacon school networks, research networks, partnerships between higher education institutions and schools and the specialist schools movement to name just some of those available. The National College for School Leadership will develop and 'spin off' further networks, often for heads whose schools share similar characteristics. There is no single, best model. What matters is that all schools break out of isolation and introversion and constantly work with and learn from others, as many already do. This is a crucial part of the teaching profession taking control of the reform agenda.

6.34 Sometimes partnerships and networks will reach out of the education service and out of the country too. Many schools are now working closely with businesses. Examples include the specialist schools and Education Action Zones which have business sponsors, the business mentoring programme for headteachers organised by Business in the Community and the Adopt-a-School arrangement that Nottingham City Education Authority has developed with its local business community.

6.35 Links outside the country to schools and teachers elsewhere are also increasingly influential. The growing numbers of teachers in our teacher exchange programme, for example, will encourage genuine links with schools elsewhere. The teacher organisations through their international counterparts are also fostering an international perspective, as are the proposals of the British Council and the European Union. Many forward-thinking schools are building partnerships with schools elsewhere which offer enhanced opportunities for pupils and teachers and also enable sharing of best practice and a deeper understanding of what world class standards of performance really are. Again the National College for School Leadership will become a key driver of progress in this area.

Parents

6.36 Perhaps most importantly, though, parents and carers have an essential role to play in education. Particularly for the youngest children, parents' involvement in and support for their child's learning is critical. That is why so many of our programmes, from Sure Start onwards are designed to support not only children but also their parents and carers in bringing up the children, and why we are supporting family learning in so many contexts.

6.37 As children grow older, parental involvement remains critical. At its most basic, parents are responsible for ensuring that their child arrives at school on time and ready to learn. But most parents want to go well beyond that in supporting their child. To do so, they most importantly need good information.

6.38 New legislation has required all Local Education Authorities to publish booklets showing for every school in their area the school's details and admission arrangements, whether demand for its places has tended to exceed supply, and how it decides which applications to accept if this happens.

6.39 In addition, we have already improved the published school performance tables, so that it is easier for parents to evaluate schools. We are committed to supplementing these improved tables further, with information about how far schools help their pupils to progress between the stages of their education (value added). We intend to do this as soon as we have the necessary information about individual pupil performance and have tested successfully the processes involved. The first value added measures – for secondary schools – will appear in the performance tables in 2002.

6.40 We are also providing information to help parents to know what they should expect from their child's school. For example, we have developed parents' guides to the curriculum which cover all stages of schooling. 3 million copies have been ordered so far. We have also established a popular and well-regarded Internet site for parents (www.parents.dfee.gov.uk). Our homework guidelines, setting out the amount of homework that children could expect at each age, were widely welcomed. Schools have the right to expect parental support in following the guidelines, and parents have the right to expect that schools should set sensible amounts of homework as set out in those guidelines. Our home-school agreements underpin this, as well as attendance and school disciplinary policies.

6.41 Choice of school is particularly important to parents, and so we have introduced fairer ways of offering school places to pupils, so that as many parents as possible can send their children to their preferred school. We have encouraged fairness in admissions in a number of ways. Our new School Admissions Code of Practice insists that all admission decisions are made on the basis of clear, fair, objective and published admissions rules and over-subscription criteria, which must now be the subject of local consultation. We have established independent Schools Adjudicators who can consider objections to proposed admission arrangements and, if necessary, change them.

6.42 Our new admissions framework means that no school can now introduce selection by ability. And our Admissions Code of Practice encourages a range of other ways of making life easier for parents facing that critical decision on which school(s) to apply to – including common timetables and co-ordinated admissions systems. But for those parents whose applications are initially rejected, new legislation and our Code of Practice on Admission Appeals have made sure that they can get a fair hearing from an appeal panel whose members are independent of the admission authority.

6.43 While some schools continue to have many more applications than places, there will inevitably be parents who do not get the outcome they want. A process as critical to children's future as choosing a school can never be stress-free for parents. But we believe that the local collaborative forum and the improved Code have made a real difference, and achieved a measurable improvement in parental satisfaction with both the outcomes and the process since the Audit Commission reported 1 in 5 dissatisfied in 1996.

6.44 We will continue to monitor the impact of the new arrangements and improve them where needed. In some areas there is still scope for better management and co-ordination of admissions operations, and better ways of avoiding the concentration of the most disadvantaged pupils in the least popular schools. We would like to be able to address the dissatisfaction that still exists in some parts of the country.

6.45 Other proposals in this Paper will promote greater parental satisfaction. Parents already have the right to express a preference for any school they wish, and to have that preference met unless other children have a better claim to the places. But we recognise that not all parents want the same things from a school; our proposals on increasing diversity should help ensure that more parents find the type of school that particularly suits their child. Sometimes, too many parents want the same school because they perceive wide variations in local school quality; our proposals to transform secondary education should make every school a school parents will be proud to send their children to.

Governors

6.46 The capacity of schools to improve and change depends not just on their staff but also on their governors. Governors have always had an important role to play in schools. That importance has increased as more power, responsibility and funding have been devolved to schools. Most recently, it has been enhanced by the introduction of school-level target-setting in 1998 and performance management for heads and teachers in 2000.

6.47 The Government recently published a consultation paper on school governance which took account of these changes in the functions of governing bodies. At the heart of the paper is the Government's belief in the importance of the role.

6.48 The consultation paper asks for views on ways in which we can help governors to do their job as effectively as possible. It suggests that governors can be freed from some executive duties, and the paperwork that goes with them, and focus more on the strategic and creative role of setting the overall direction and mission of the school. It suggests a streamlining of governing bodies, so that they work as effectively as possible in this role.

6.49 We are also consulting on proposals to allow governing bodies to group and work together if this would support higher standards. This could be beneficial particularly if it brings small primaries together to exploit economies of scale, pairs selective and non-selective schools together, brings weaker schools into a cluster with stronger ones or supports transition by bringing a secondary and its feeder primaries together.

6.50 We are also looking at ways of improving training and administrative support for governing bodies, so that governors are better able to be effective and we will continue to invest substantial resources in governor training. We are also committed to improving the supply of effective school governors, including by piloting a range of ideas in Excellence in Cities areas. The new concept of a one-stop shop for those interested in becoming governors is beginning to work. Already this service has provided some 640 governors for schools in challenging circumstances. Finally, we are also proposing strengthened powers to intervene when schools fail.

6.51 Taken together, these measures are intended to support governors and strengthen governing bodies in their key role of supporting heads, teachers and other staff to raise standards in schools.

Local Education Authorities

6.52 Local Education Authorities have an important, clearly-defined and continuing role in supporting schools to raise standards. How that role is defined has changed dramatically over recent years. Local Education Authorities no longer control schools but they do have a key role in challenging and supporting them.

6.53 The recent DfEE policy paper *The role of the Local Education Authority in school education* summarises the role of the Local Education Authority under five key headings:

- Special Educational Needs.
- Access and school transport.
- School improvement and tackling failure.
- Educating excluded pupils and pupil welfare.
- Strategic management – for example of resources, including allocation of funds between schools, of assets (through our introduction of Asset Management Plans), admissions and initiatives such as Excellence in Cities.

6.54 Where schools are succeeding, they should not be subject to interference, but given the freedom to build on their success. Where schools are coasting, they need to be challenged to improve; where they are in danger of failing, intervention must be swift, decisive and effective. That is our principle of intervention in inverse proportion to success. As a source of local accountability, Authorities are well-placed to put that principle into practice. And we changed the law in 1998 to allow us to intervene in Local Education Authorities if that was indicated by the inspection evidence. The evidence suggests that Education Authorities are becoming increasingly effective in carrying out their role: OFSTED's analysis shows improved standards of performance among them and the fall, not just in the numbers of failing schools in total, but in the numbers going into special measures term by term, is encouraging. All the signs are that Local Authorities have recognised and acted upon their duty to raise standards.

6.55 There are services too that it makes no sense for schools to provide alone. Home-to-school transport, planning the supply of school places in an area and the co-ordination of SEN services are important examples. Major economies of scale and improved co-ordination of services result from carrying out this work across a Local Authority rather than at a school level, and these will continue to be an important part of Local Education Authority work.

6.56 The Government will continue to develop further ways of identifying and disseminating good Local Education Authority practice. In doing so it will work with OFSTED and the local authority associations.

6.57 We will also continue to tackle inadequate performance by Local Education Authorities through direct support and intervention, where this proves necessary. More importantly we want to encourage and support all authorities to ask fundamental questions about how best to carry out their Local Education Authority role in the 21st century. Clearly they need to operate within a framework that ensures the quality of all their services. The lack of professional standards for school improvement services and those who work within them is, for example, a key weakness of the current arrangements, and one which could hold back the pace of reform.

6.58 To encourage more rapid and imaginative progress, we have suggested four further practical ways for Authorities to build on recent reforms and pursue modernisation. These activities reinforce each other and are designed to operate together:

- Education Authorities can help to promote a more open market in schools' services and take steps to ensure that all schools have the knowledge and skills they need to be better purchasers of goods and services.
- Education Authorities can test out new ways of sharing school improvement responsibilities with groups of schools who have the knowledge and skills to discharge that role.
- Education Authorities can develop and trial new ways of discharging responsibilities in partnership with other Local Authorities, and with other public-private and voluntary sector bodies.
- We are also working on the development of national professional standards and national recognition of those engaged in the key role of school improvement.

These four key proposals for action are set out in more detail in *The role of the Local Education Authority in school education,* which was published in the autumn of 2000. We are supporting a range of developments involving Education Authorities and partners to promote innovation in these areas.

6.59 Education Authorities also have a key part to play in linking education to other services and building partnerships to reduce social exclusion. Reducing social exclusion requires problem-solving collaboration between various aspects of the public service, including Local Authorities. Sure Start is one example of what is possible. Education Action Zones and Excellence in Cities are others. For example, Education Action Zones, such as that in Wythenshawe in Manchester, involve health, social and police services alongside education in tackling the problems of particular areas. In Hertfordshire, the Local Authority has created a new Children, Schools and Families service to provide a fully integrated approach to meeting the needs of children and families. By unifying its casework practices, developing local preventative strategies and building capacity in schools, the new service is aligned to local health, public and voluntary sector provision. These developments are crucial, not least because raising educational standards is central to local regeneration, promoting health and the revival of communities. For example, the recent rapid improvement of the education service in Liverpool has gone hand in hand with regeneration of the city itself.

6.60 While schools will continue to be the key driving force for raising standards, there is no doubt that the improved capacity of Education Authorities, across this range of tasks, is the key to creating a context within which schools can succeed.

Capacity at the Centre

6.61 The reforms since 1997 have been driven from central Government. This was necessary in order to generate a new sense of urgency, to create a new culture focused firmly on standards and to demonstrate that step-change in pupil performance was not only possible but could be achieved rapidly. The creation of the Standards and Effectiveness Unit in the DfEE was an important part of that, as was the continuation and extension of the role of OFSTED.

6.62 Many lessons have been learnt from this phase about the delivery of major reform. It does require sustained priority and a clear focus. It does involve serious, steady investment. It does depend on putting in place a dedicated infrastructure which can deliver effectively, whether through regional directors in the case of literacy and numeracy at primary level or partnerships at local level in the case of early years or Excellence in Cities. It does demand high-quality, ongoing professional development for all those involved in implementation. It does require strategies which are universal, and therefore include the entire service, but are also targeted and therefore provide most support where the challenge is greatest. Finally, any significant reform will only become irreversible if it is pursued consistently for several years.

6.63 We will apply the lessons learned from the last four years in the future. For example, the approach to lower secondary education reform will draw on the lessons of success at primary level but be refined and adapted to take account of the greater complexity of the secondary school and curriculum.

6.64 At the broader level, it was always the intention, once the culture had begun to change and success was evident across the system, that schools and teachers, at the frontline, would play an increasing part in reform. In a rapidly changing world, only by encouraging innovation at school level will the education system be able to keep up with other sectors. Moreover, the systematic application of the principle of intervention in inverse proportion to success implies, by definition, that as the system improves Government will need to intervene less. We should increasingly see schools which earn greater autonomy and reward in return for demonstrating good performance.

6.65 As this occurs, the role of Government will not become less important but it will change. Its key functions will be:

- To provide leadership by spelling out the vision and the targets the service should achieve.
- To set education within the wider context of social and economic change.
- To establish the regulatory and accountability framework within which increasingly autonomous schools play their part.
- To design strategies for reform that enable successful change.
- To celebrate success and draw attention to the role of education in society as a whole so that parents and communities recognise its importance and respect teachers and other staff in schools for the contribution they make.
- To monitor the progress of the system at every level and intervene on behalf of the pupils wherever necessary.
- To learn constantly from schools, teachers and others who work in education what is working well and what is working less well and adjust policies accordingly.
- Last but not least, to invest steadily and consistently in education over several years in order to create a favourable context for change.

Performing these roles will require Government to change the way it works. Above all, it will need to build on the progress that has been made to become more in touch, outward-facing and responsive.

6.66 Implied in this changing role is a new sense of partnership. It is perfectly possible to create a world class education service in this country. Doing so depends on a number of things, not least the successful implementation of the reforms set out in this Paper. But above all, it depends on creating between educators, parents, communities and business, and Government, a powerful partnership committed to the achievement of the highest possible standards for every child and young person. We believe that the education service and our society are now ready to make that commitment.

We welcome your views on this Green Paper. Copies of the full paper, a summary version and the response form are available on the DfEE website at www.dfee.gov.uk/buildingonsuccess. Alternatively they can be ordered free of charge along with Braille and audio versions by ringing 0845 60 222 60 and quoting references: DfEE 0041/2001 for the full version; DfEE 0042/2001 for the summary; and DfEE 0054/2001 for the response form, or by e-mailing dfee@prolog.uk.com.

You are invited to complete the response form online, return it by e-mail to Green.Paper@dfee.gov.uk or send it by post (including taped responses) to:

DfEE School Green Paper Response Unit
4T Sanctuary Buildings
Great Smith Street
London
SW1P 3BT

Tel: 020 7925 5560 (response form queries only)
Fax: 020 7925 5570

Under the Code of Practice on Open Government, any responses will be made available to the public on request, unless respondents indicate that they wish their response to remain confidential. The consultation period runs until 1 June 2001. The Paper relates to England only.

Printed in the UK for The Stationery Office Limited
On behalf of the Controller of Her Majesty's Stationery Office
Dd5069787 2/01 025038 TJ003587